EMQs for the MRCOG

John Duthie and Paul Hodges

EMQs for the MRCOG

A Guide to Extended Matching Questions for the MRCOG Part 1 Examination

First published 2007

ISBN 978-1-904752-43-1

Published by the RCOG Press
at the Royal College of Obstetricians
and Gynaecologists
27 Sussex Place, Regent's Park
London NW1 4RG

www.rcog.org.uk

Registered Charity No. 213280

RCOG Press Editor: Jane Moody

Text designed & typeset at the Typographic Design Unit

Indexing by Liza Furnival

Printed in the United Kingdom by Latimer Trend & Co. Ltd

Contents

Preface

Both the Part 1 and Part 2 examinations leading to Membership of the Royal College of Obstetricians and Gynaecologists are continuing to undergo change at the present time. While the amendments are gradual, cumulatively they amount to a significant change in the examining process. Extending matching questions (EMQs) have an important place in the evolution of these examinations. They were introduced as a component of the written paper of the Part 2 MRCOG examination in September 2006 and, with effect from September 2007, EMQs are also being introduced to the Part 1 MRCOG examination.

The purpose of the change to the Part 1 examination is to introduce an additional format of testing which probes a candidate's understanding of the subject more deeply than true/false multiple choice questions (MCQs) and tests their understanding of the inter-relationships between facts in the relevant basic and clinical sciences. Their combination with the more traditional MCQs enables adequate coverage of the syllabus and should increase the overall validity of the examination without sacrificing its current reliability.

Both of us have contributed to the continuing development of both the Part 1 and Part 2 MRCOG examinations. We have worked with colleagues in order to develop, discuss and refine EMQs for both parts of the examination. We have written this book to assist doctors in their preparation for success in an examination that is designed to measure their understanding of basic and clinical sciences as applied to the fascinating field of obstetrics and gynaecology. Whether an individual doctor ultimately becomes a clinician or pursues a career in research, a sound knowledge and understanding of the underpinning science is of fundamental importance.

We trust that you will find our book helpful and we wish you a successful entry to an enthralling specialty.

Mr S J Duthie MB ChB (Liverpool) Dip Ven (Liverpool) FRCOG
Consultant Obstetrician and Gynaecologist
Blackpool, Fylde and Wyre Hospitals NHS Trust

Dr P D Hodges BA (Hons) DPhil
Deputy to Head of Examinations Department
Royal College of Obstetricians and Gynaecologists

About the authors

John Duthie is a Consultant Obstetrician and Gynaecologist at the Blackpool, Fylde and Wyre Hospitals NHS Trust. He graduated in medicine at Liverpool University and took up a Lectureship in Obstetrics and Gynaecology at the University of Hong Kong, followed by posts as Senior Registrar in Liverpool and Chester. He was appointed a full-time consultant in 1995. For many years he has been passionate about medical education; he was appointed as an examiner for the Diploma of the RCOG in 1997 and for the MRCOG in 2001. He served on the Part 2 EMQ committee from its inception in 2003 to 2006. He has taught on several of the MRCOG revision courses and has been co-convener of the College's Part 2 revision course since 2005. In March 2007 he was sponsored by the College to visit and liaise with the National Board of Medical Examiners in Philadelphia, USA, on item development and assessment of test validity. This is his third co-authored textbook and he has many publications in peer-reviewed journals.

Paul Hodges has worked in the Examination Department of the College since 2003 and has been Deputy to the Head of the Department since April 2006. From 2000 to 2003 he worked in a similar capacity at the Institute of Healthcare Management. He completed a part-time PhD in First World War history in 2007 and is hoping to publish a resultant book soon. This is his second book co-authored with John and he is active in assessment and medical education research and publication.

Acknowledgements

We would like to thank Dr Michael Murphy, Director of Education, Royal College of Obstetricians and Gynaecologists, for his continued inspiration, wisdom and vision. We would also like to thank Professor William Ledger, Chair of the Examinations and Assessment Committee, Royal College of Obstetricians and Gynaecologists, for his support and for writing the Foreword to this book. Finally, we also acknowledge the outstanding effort of Professor Alison Fiander, Current Chair of the Part I Examination Committee and the present and past members of that Committee in enabling the new and improved examination to take place.

Abbreviations

CREST	calcinosis, Raynaud phenomenon, esophageal dysmotility, sclerodactyly, and telangiectasia
EMQ	extended matching question
K^+	potassium
MCQ	multiple choice question (in this context generally refers to the true/false format)
Na^+	sodium
T/F	true or false (a format of MCQ requiring one of the two answers)
MRCOG	Member of the Royal College of Obstetricians and Gynaecologists
RCOG	Royal College of Obstetricians and Gynaecologists
ST1	Year 1 of specialist training

Foreword

As Chairman of the Examination Committee at the RCOG, a question I am quite frequently asked is, 'Why is the Part 1 MRCOG a basic and clinical sciences examination?' An underlying subtext often seems to be, 'What is the point of this exam?' Medical science is growing faster than ever. Investigations and treatments derived from the 'new' bioscience of the 1980s and 1990s are now impacting upon clinical practice. Clinical consultants are being asked to use these tools properly and to advise patients of their utility. An increasingly cost-conscious NHS and other worldwide healthcare systems under pressure require that they be used only when necessary.

How to equip the consultants of the future to deal with these pressures? Senior clinicians need to be able to engage in informed discussion with the scientific innovators, to understand the opportunities and limitations of new techniques and tools in medicine and to be confident when appraising new technologies. This confidence can only follow from an adequate grounding in clinical science.

Even a cursory look at developments in obstetrics and gynaecology over the last 30 years – the length of time over which we expect consultant colleagues to practise – demonstrates the extent to which the technological revolution has already changed our specialty. Ultrasound, laparoscopy, in vitro fertilisation, fetal blood sampling and prenatal diagnosis are now all used in day-to-day clinical practice. None was in widespread use when our senior colleagues were newly appointed consultants. Molecular biology and genetics now have clinical applications in prenatal diagnosis, gynaecological oncology and reproductive medicine, and advances in gene therapy and stem cell science will undoubtedly be translated into practice in the next decade. Clinical epidemiology and statistics, and understanding of clinical risk, are other relatively new concepts that are deeply embedded within clinical practice.

The aim of the Part 1 MRCOG should be to guide candidates to learn the important aspects of biological science as relevant to the practice of obstetrics and gynaecology. Without this knowledge base, the gap between scientist and clinician will grow still wider and we clinicians will neither be able to apply new developments in biosciences intelligently nor be able to counsel patients adequately. Medicine and science are inextricably linked and new recruits to the ranks of obstetrics and gynaecology should attain a reasonable basic knowledge to prepare them for a life of constant change and innovation.

In due course, progress to further specialist training will be determined by the demonstration of specified competencies expressly linked to the curriculum for initial specialist training and confirmed by completion of a range of assessments, including Part 1 of the Membership examination. In the meantime, Professor Alison Fiander, the current chair of the Part 1 MRCOG subcommittee, a not undemanding post, and I speak from personal experience and her hardworking committee has made great progress in a number of areas:

- adopting a new, explicit syllabus
- improving the quality and clinical relevance of the examination questions (MCQs) and item bank:
  - 20–30% of questions depending on category have been removed from the current item bank and many more have been revised to bring them up to date and to remove abstruse knowledge
  - the number of questions on anatomy, physiology and biochemistry have been reduced in favour of questions on clinical trials, clinical statistics and epidemiology
- clarifying the examination's positioning – within the UK, candidates to be encouraged to take the examination after Foundation Year 2 and required to pass the examination before exit from the ST1 component of their training
- improving the examination's standard setting – now undertaken by a well-trained group comprising new Members of the College (who have passed Part 2 MRCOG within the last 5 years) and clinical lecturers in obstetrics and gynaecology, coordinated in collaboration with the RCOG Trainees' Committee.

The introduction of a number of EMQs into the Part 1 examination is another important step in this story of progression. Having seen their heartening success in the Part 2 Membership examination recently, they should prove to be to the advantage of good candidates. This book, with some well-rounded revision of the medical sciences so important to the effective practice of obstetrics and gynaecology, should help candidates become good candidates. Clearing the hurdle of the Part 1 MRCOG is the first, important step in a good candidate becoming a future good consultant obstetrician and gynaecologist – which is a very good thing to be.

Professor William Ledger
Chair, RCOG Examination Committee

How to use this book

The first two chapters provide some background and an introduction to the new format and will help you to decide how best to approach this examination. The next chapter, Chapter 3, provides worked examples of specimen EMQs with answers and a brief explanation. In total there are eight lists of options and 28 twigs. There is also some advice on how to tackle each EMQ and how to avoid mistakes.

Chapters 4 and 5 are two mock full papers: examples of exactly what candidates will face in the full 2-hour written papers of the Part 1 MRCOG examination. These mock full papers also mirror the examination's subject areas so that Chapter 4 covers Paper 1 and Chapter 5 covers Paper 2. To make it an exact replica of the examination to be faced you should recreate examination conditions as best as you can (at the very least, make sure you cannot be disturbed at all) and time yourself tackling it – under 2 hours should be your target.

Chapters 6–9 inclusive are other mock papers concentrating on the EMQ format. These are again split into the Paper 1 and Paper 2 subject areas alternating. There are ten option lists in each, again producing a total of 20 questions. These papers should provide you with an even more realistic trial of what the new EMQ sections of the Part 1 papers will be like.

The answers to all the 'mock' papers are given at the back of this book in Chapters 10–15, as follows:

- Chapter 4 answers will be found in Chapter 10
- Chapter 5 answers will be found in Chapter 11
- Chapter 6 answers will be found in Chapter 12
- Chapter 7 answers will be found in Chapter 13
- Chapter 8 answers will be found in Chapter 14
- Chapter 9 answers will be found in Chapter 15.

Appendix 1 provides filled-in answer keys to the mock examinations. This will allow you to easily tally your number of correct answers and your number of incorrect answers. When reviewing your performance in the mock examinations it is a good idea to make quite detailed notes on the option lists and questions that you answered incorrectly so that you can guide your future revision.

When reviewing your performance in the mock examinations, it is a good idea to make quite detailed notes on the option lists and questions that you answered incorrectly to guide your future revision.

Also included at the back of the book is a fold-out blank answer sheet (Appendix 2) for you to use when attempting the mock papers. This is only section of the book not subject to copyright. Please photocopy the sheet for easier and repeated use.

1 | The educational and evaluative benefits of EMQs

It is worth briefly covering the College's intentions in introducing this new question format to the Part 1 examination papers, and its educational and evaluative benefits. Basic knowledge of these purposes should aid candidates' preparation for this new style of question. A lot more detail on the preparations made by the College and the ethos behind the new examination can be found in the article on which this chapter is based.[1]

There are a number of compelling reasons promoting the introduction of EMQs for the College. They:

- are relatively easy to write well
- can be computer marked with unerring accuracy
- are a form of examination that will increase the validity and reliability of our overall assessment of candidates
- can test more complex understanding of knowledge than MCQs
- allow Part 1 questions to be constructed that are more readily relevant or applicable to clinical practice.

EMQs are now widely and successfully used in undergraduate-level medical examinations and have started to be used at postgraduate level. The Royal College of Psychiatrists introduced EMQs in the Spring 2003 sitting of the Part 1 MRCPsych examination, following encouraging results in a pilot paper. They have been successfully used in the membership examination of the Royal College of Surgeons (Glasgow and London) and Royal College of General Practitioners. Also, the Royal College of Paediatrics and Child Health uses EMQs in its Diploma in Child Health. The PLAB test is entirely in EMQ format. The RCOG introduced a 40-item, 1-hour EMQ paper to the Part 2 MRCOG written examination from September 2006. Although, at the time of writing, the Part 2 EMQs have only been run in trials and at one 'real' sitting, thus lacking longitudinal data to thoroughly support great confidence, early data suggest that the format is performing very well. As the College hoped, based on the educational literature, EMQs have so far proved to be excellent discriminators.[2] Candidates performing well overall in the Part 2 written examination generally achieved high marks on the EMQ paper and candidates performing poorly overall received low marks. At a more individual level, each question's statistical measure of discrimination (Pearson point biserial) was good. Indeed, every single EMQ-format question had a positive point biserial, indicating that it was discriminating in the correct way. Even taking into account the in-built advantage of rather higher weighting,[3] Part 2 EMQs comfortably outperformed the MCQs of the same examination sitting at discriminating between high- and low-performing candidates.[1] With good writing techniques now embedded within the College, there is no reason to believe that the new Part 1 EMQs cannot emulate their clinic-based predecessors. This should produce a more sophisticated and relevant examination which is also fairer to borderline candidates, thus improving validity and reliability of the Part 1 examination. Educational research clearly indicates that examinations, particularly those with a high stake such as the Part 1 MRCOG, are improved by increasing the number of performance indicators through increasing the number of test formats.[4] As an aside, it should be noted that the quality of questions provided by many commercial online revision websites and courses is far below those used by the College.

EMQs will drive the learning required to pass the Part 1 MRCOG in a slightly different way than the current question formats. However, the impact should be less dramatic than has been the case at the Part 2 level. Essentially, for Part 1, the same knowledge as before will be tested but with greater integration and depth.

Perhaps the most important message though is not to worry too much. EMQs, after all, will currently only contribute 20% of your overall mark in the Part 1 examination.

REFERENCES

1. Duthie SJ, Fiander A, Hodges PD. Extended matching questions: a new component of the Part 1 examination leading to Membership of the Royal College of Obstetricians and Gynaecologists. *The Obstetrician & Gynaecologist* 2007; **9(3)**: (in press).

2. Duthie SJ, Hodges PD, Ramsay I, Reid W. EMQs: a new component of the MRCOG Part 2 exam. *The Obstetrician & Gynaecologist* 2006; **8**: 181–5.

3. Royal College of Obstetricians and Gynaecologists. A new format for the Part 2 MRCOG written examination [www.rcog.org.uk/index.asp?PageID =1338].

4. Linn RL. Assessments and accountability. *Educational Researcher* 2000; **29**: 4–12.

2 | EMQ answering technique

Introduction

Before you attempt to take the Part I examination leading to Membership of the Royal College of Obstetricians and Gynaecologists you should have a thorough knowledge of basic sciences as applied to the specialty. You should be familiar with the current syllabus, in both its summary[1] and matrix[2] formats. The latter, with its cross-matching to the Core Curriculum in Obstetrics and Gynaecology, is particularly useful for revision planning. Up until March 2007 the Part I examination was composed of two papers and each paper comprised 300 MCQs.

The purpose of adding the EMQ format is their ability to probe a candidate's understanding of a subject. EMQs assess the application of knowledge and they also test the understanding of the relationships between different facts. MCQs are also extremely reliable in terms of producing results that are consistent. However, concern has been expressed that MCQs simply test the isolated recall of facts. EMQs are replacing a number of the MCQs in both Paper I and Paper 2 of the Part I examination. With effect from September 2007, each of the papers contains 240 MCQs and 20 EMQs. It is recognised that the EMQs take longer to read, cerebration (it is hoped) takes longer and several of the questions contain functional distracters. With these issues in mind, each correct score for an EMQ item gains three marks, compared with just one mark for each correct MCQ answer. Thus, with 240 MCQs and 20 EMQs, the total score for each paper remains 300.

A candidate with a sound knowledge of the basic and clinical sciences relevant to obstetrics and gynaecology should have little difficulty in tackling EMQs. However, failure to appreciate the relationship between knowledge and technique may affect your performance in the examination. Essentially, both your knowledge and examination technique should be sound.

The purpose of the EMQ is to increase the validity of the test by asking questions around a scientific or clinical scenario. Although several of the EMQs demand thorough knowledge, many will require the candidate to think through the data that are presented. In this manner, the EMQ may revolve around a pregnant woman in the clinic. Other EMQs revolve around scientific data, laboratory findings or statistical data. They tend to assess your medical knowledge rather deeper than simple recall and there will be several options to deter guessing.

Attributes of EMQs

So what are the main differences between EMQs and these more familiar formats of assessment?

With the wider number of options available, it is obvious that the educated guess becomes a far less valuable technique than in the 50 : 50 world of the true or false MCQ. Studies demonstrate that, even in negatively marked MCQ papers, all candidates should benefit substantially from backing their educated guesses and only a small percentage lose marks by backing their wild guesses.[3] That doesn't mean that an educated guess is not sometimes appropriate for EMQs. The popular and renowned advice to go with the first answer you think of first seems to be gaining ever more support. The RCOG MCQ and EMQ papers are not negatively marked, making the technique potentially even more potent. Essentially, for the EMQ format questions your guessing needs to be judicious. This book therefore provides much advice on the best strategy for minimising your risk of answering incorrectly and maximising your possible score. Each worked example covers this topic. As with the true/false MCQ paper, there is no negative marking. However, even 'good guessing' may well lead to an unsustainably high number of mistakes in the EMQ section of the paper. While Part 1 EMQs will not reach the levels of synthesis of clinical knowledge that can be tested in the Part 2 written examination, especially its EMQs, they do test more complex understanding of basic science than MCQs. Simple knowledge recall suffices for correctly answering many true/false MCQs. This will continue to apply to many Part 1 EMQs as well, although some will require working through. Solid, applied, scientific knowledge will be required to tackle many of the Part 1 EMQs. A number will have quite substantial scenarios to interpret. In recognition of their increased length and complexity, in particular with regard to the extra time required to read them, EMQs have been assigned a longer time for completion than MCQs. It is important to bear this in mind when preparing for the examination. However, most Part 1 EMQs will be much shorter than the heavily clinical scenarios of the Part 1 EMQ paper.

The structure of an EMQ is as follows:

- a list of options
- lead-in statement or paragraph
- the items.

The number of options on the list will vary from a minimum of three up to a maximum of 20. There are thus 20 spaces lettered *A* to *T* to fill in on the answer sheet (see our example provided for the mock examinations in this book). The majority of questions in the examination will have around 10–14 options in their lists. As far as reasonably possible, the list of options is made homogeneous: that is, most options will be broadly equivalent or at least in similar areas. The option lists will nearly always be in alphabetical or numerical order for ease of reference; if not, they will be in the most appropriate order for quick reference.

Candidates should find this technique useful in tackling EMQs:

1. Read the 'lead-in' statement first.
2. Ask yourself the question, 'Do I really understand what the lead-in statement says?'
3. Consider each item one by one.
4. Develop the answer to the item in your mind.
5. Finally, select the correct answer from the list of options and enter your answer into the mark sheet.

We would advise candidates not to read through the list of options before reading the lead-in statement. There is a small but live possibility that you may receive a misleading cue from a 'functional distracter' among the list of options – especially if it is a subject of which you are not completely sure. The lead-in statements should leave no room for ambiguity. The tasks that are to be performed would be explained very clearly. Reading the lead-in statement and comprehending it will be the key to performing the task required in the correct manner and thus maximising your score. Most candidates would find EMQs easy to deal with. Consider Worked Example 1, taken from a totally different area than obstetrics and gynaecology, so there are no unnecessary distractions.

WORKED EXAMPLE 1

Options

A Beijing
B Datong
C Kyoto
D Nagoya
E Nagasaki
F Nara
G Osaka
H Pyongyang
I Seoul
J Shanghai
K Tokyo
L Xiamen
M Xian
N Yokohama

Instructions

The list of options refers to cities in the Far East. Select the **single** city that matches the description in each of the items listed below. Each option may be used once, more than once or not at all.

Item 1 ▶ The **current** capital city of Japan.
Answer ▷ *K*=Tokyo.

Item2 ▶ The capital city of Japan during the period between AD 794 and AD 1180.
Answer ▷ *C*=Kyoto.

Item 3 ▶ The capital city of Japan during the period between AD 710 and AD 740.
Answer ▷ *F*=Nara.

Commentary

The lead-in statement states clearly that the list of options relates to cities in the Far East. A close examination of the list of options actually shows that the cities are selected from Japan, South Korea and China. The list of items is homogenous. There are no cities from North America, Europe or India. The candidate is asked to select the city which matches the description that is provided in the items below. This question tests a candidate's knowledge of current and previous capital cities of Japan. The current capital city of Japan is Tokyo and this fact is commonly known. The second question introduces another element – what was the capital city in Japan during a specific period of time? The answer is Kyoto and you would need a through knowledge of Japanese history in order to answer this question correctly. Arguably, even fewer people would know that the capital city of Japan during an even earlier time period was Nara.

Consider the next example, again taken from a different area than obstetrics and gynaecology.

WORKED EXAMPLE 2

Options

	Ratio of body to tail	Bare area of skin over the mandible	Native wild populations
A	Body and tail of similar lengths	Yes	South America
B	Body and tail of similar lengths	Yes	India
C	Body and tail of similar lengths	No	South America
D	Body is much longer than tail	Yes	Australia
E	Body is much longer than tail	Yes	Russia
F	Body is much shorter than the tail	No	Canada

Instructions

The list of options provides descriptions of birds by the ratio of length of body to length of tail, whether or not they have the morphological feature of a bare area of skin around the mandible and the geographical locations of native wild populations. Select the **single** correct profile for each of the birds in the items below. Each option may be used once, more than once or not at all.

Item 1 ▶ Blue-and-gold macaw.
Answer ▷ *A.*

Item 2 ▶ Hyacinth macaw.
Answer ▷ *A.*

Item 3 ▶ Black palm cockatoo.
Answer ▷ *D.*

Commentary

You are likely to meet a 'table' in some of the lists of options in the actual examination. In this particular example, the list of options provides different profiles of different birds. The lead-in statement describes – very clearly – what is required of the candidate. A macaw parrot is a bird that has two characteristics: a bare area of skin around the mandible and the ratio of body to tail is one to one. Both features are seen in a macaw parrot. The EMQ also tests one's knowledge of where these birds are found in the wild. Blue-and-gold and hyacinth macaws are simply two different types of macaw parrot. Why is '*B*' not a possible answer? Macaw parrots are found in the wild in South America. Therefore, the answer must be '*A*'. Similarly, the black palm cockatoo has a body which is much longer than its tail, has a bare area of skin over the face and is found in Australia. This EMQ shows that it is possible to test the knowledge of morphological characteristics of a bird together with knowledge of its geographical distribution using a single question.

Enough about current and previous capital cities of Japan and parrots. What about the Part I MRCOG examination? We have provided some examples of the sorts of lists of options which are being developed for the Part I MRCOG examination in this book. The following are examples of the types of additional lists that will be used:

- types of inheritance of genetic disorders
- enzyme defects in genetic disorders
- biochemical reactions
- immunological reactions
- acid-base disorders
- embryological origin of organs and tissues
- anatomic connections of organs
- blood supply of organs
- biochemical actions of hormones
- physiological effects of hormones
- different type of haemoglobinopathy
- effect of drugs on physiological variables
- adverse effects of drugs
- different values for standard deviation and standard error (derivable using simple calculations)
- transport proteins and their ligands
- pathogenic micro-organisms
- profiles (see worked examples)
- different types of membrane transport systems.

Pass marks

Unfortunately, it is too early to know what sort of pass marks will be set for the Part 1 paper with EMQ format added. Anyway, these will, of course, vary owing to standard setting. However, as guesswork plays a far lower role in EMQs than MCQs it is almost inconceivable that the high pass marks of the traditional true/false MCQ paper, generally in the region of

78–81%, will be duplicated, although obviously with only 20% of the questions being EMQs this will not be modulated that greatly. For the Part 2 EMQ paper, we estimated before launch a rough range of pass mark somewhere between 55% and 70%, with the region of 62–67% being likely. In fact, the standard set pass mark for the first sitting was 60%. However, we do not think that the Part 1 EMQs will be quite as challenging as the Part 2 ones. An overall pass mark in the range of 73–79% is likely (that is, around 78–81% on the MCQs and 64–70% on the EMQs); 77% perhaps should be aimed at as a likely pass mark.

REFERENCES

1. Royal College of Obstetricians and Gynaecologists. Part 1 MRCOG syllabus summary [www.rcog.org.uk/index.asp?PageID =174].

2. Royal College of Obstetricians and Gynaecologists. Part One and Core Curriculum Matrix [www.rcog.org.uk/index.asp?pageID =1912].

3. Hammond EJ, McIndoe AK, Sansome AJ, Spargo PM. Multiple-choice examinations: adopting an evidence-based approach to exam technique. *Anaesthesia* 1998; **53**: 1105–8.

3 | Worked examples

OPTION LIST I

Theme ▶ Understanding measurement and manipulation

Domain ▶ Research

Options

A	2 mmHg	H	9 mmHg
B	3 mmHg	I	10 mmHg
C	4 mmHg	J	16 mmHg
D	5 mmHg	K	25 mmHg
E	6 mmHg	L	30 mmHg
F	7 mmHg	M	31 mmHg
G	8 mmHg	N	32 mmHg

Instructions

For each of the studies below, calculate and select the **single** most appropriate standard deviation from the list of options. Each of the studies refer to systolic blood pressure in normal healthy pregnant women, the measurements of systolic blood pressure show a perfect Gaussian distribution and N = the number of women in each study. Each option may be used once, more than once or not at all.

Item 1 ▶ N = 5000, mean = 100 mmHg, variance = 9.
Answer ▷ B = 3 mmHg.

Item 2 ▶ N = 50, mean = 105 mmHg, variance = 64.
Answer ▷ G = 8 mmHg.

Item 3 ▶ N = 500, mean = 110 mmHg, variance = 16.
Answer ▷ C = 4 mmHg.

Commentary

Purpose

The purpose of this EMQ is to test your understanding of standard deviation and variance.

Content

In this EMQ the each of the items refers clearly to a numerical value with the units 'mmHg'. The lead-in statement explains that each of the items refers to a study in which the systolic blood pressure in normal healthy pregnant women was measured. It is explained very clearly that the distribution of the measurements of systolic blood pressure show a perfect Gaussian (normal) distribution and that $N =$ the number of women in each study. The candidate is asked to calculate the standard deviation in each study and select the correct answer from the list of options.

Answers

In a Gaussian distribution, the standard deviation is equal to the square root of the variance. You can see that the number of women in each study N and the value of the mean serve merely as functional distracters. Applying the very simple formula you would derive the answers as follows:

Item 1 = B ▶ 3 mmHg.

Item 2 = G ▶ 8 mmHg.

Item 3 = C ▶ 4 mmHg.

Minimising the risk and maximising your score

For all the questions in the examination, read the question carefully. The questions are reasonable, they test fundamental understanding of a basic subject and the formula for calculating the standard deviation from the variance is exceedingly simple. The examiners have also, thoughtfully, chosen values of variance; 9, 64 and 16, which provide easy calculations for square root. A candidate who does not understand the relationship between standard deviation and variance risks losing marks on this particular EMQ. If you do understand the subject you would be able to work out the answers to the three items without using a calculator and within a matter of seconds.

Under the stressful conditions of the actual examination a candidate is at risk of getting muddled up with numbers. There are 14 options in the option list and some candidates may inadvertently choose the wrong option.

OPTION LIST 2

Theme ▶ Obstetrics

Domain ▶ Transplacental infection

Options

	Maternal disease	Type	Risk of transplacental infection
A	Babesiosis	Protozoan	No
B	Babesiosis	Protozoan	Yes
C	Coccidioidomycosis	Fungus	No
D	Coccidioidomycosis	Fungus	Yes
E	Malaria	Bacterium	Yes
F	Malaria	Protozoan	No
G	Malaria	Protozoan	Yes
H	Malaria	Virus	Yes
I	Q fever	Rickettsia	Yes
J	Q fever	Virus	Yes
K	Schistosomiasis	Helminth	Yes
L	Schistosomiasis	Protozoan	Yes

	Maternal disease	Type	Risk of transplacental infection
M	Syphilis	Protozoan	Yes
N	Syphilis	Spirochete	No
O	Syphilis	Spirochete	Yes
P	Syphilis	Virus	Yes
Q	Tuberculosis	Bacterium	No
R	Tuberculosis	Bacterium	Yes
S	Tuberculosis	Fungus	No
T	Tuberculosis	Protozoan	No

Instructions

The list of options refers to different maternal diseases which are caused by micro-organisms, the type of organism and whether or not there is a risk of transplacental infection. Select the **single** correct profile from the list of options for each of the micro-organisms in the items below. Each option may be used once, more than once or not at all.

Item 1 ▶ Treponema pallidum.
Answer ▷ *O*=Syphilis; Spirochete; YES.

Item 2 ▶ Mycobacterium tuberculosis.
Answer ▷ *R*=Tuberculosis; Bacterium; YES.

Item 3 ▶ Plasmodium falciparum.
Answer ▷ *G*=Malaria; Protozoan; YES.

Commentary

Purpose

The purpose of this EMQ is to test a candidate's understanding of microbial illnesses during pregnancy.

Content

This particular EMQ contains a table which is incorporated into the list of options. It is important for you to become familiar with this particular format of EMQ. The lead-in statement is precise. It is clear that the list of options provides profiles of maternal disease which may be caused by micro-organisms and whether or not there is a risk of transplacental infection.

Answers

Item 1 = O ▶ Treponema pallidum causes syphilis in the mother, is a spirochete and there is a risk of transplacental infection.

Item 2 = R ▶ Mycobacterium tuberculosis is a bacterium and there is a risk of transplacental infection.

Item 3 = G ▶ Plasmodium falciparum causes malaria. It is a protozoan and there is a risk of transplacental infection.

Minimising risk and maximising your score

This is a straightforward question which tests a candidate's basic knowledge of microbiology. The answers are quite obvious and can be easily picked out from the (rather long) list of options. The pitfall here is that candidates could waste their time by reading through the whole list of options. EMQs will vary in their difficulty. A candidate with good examination technique would build up a useful bank of 'reserve time' by maintaining a good pace through questions like this.

OPTION LIST 3

Theme ▶ Biochemistry

Domain ▶ Bilirubin

Options

A Bone marrow
B Circulation
C Common bile duct
D Gastrointestinal tract distal to the entry of the common bile duct
E Gastrointestinal tract proximal to the entry of the common bile duct
F Kidney
G Liver
H Pancreas
I Portal vein
J Spleen
K Spleen, bone marrow and liver
L Stomach

Instructions

The items below refer to different stages of the metabolism of bilirubin. Select the **single** site of each reaction from the list of options. Each option may be used once, more than once or not at all.

Item 1 ▶ Conversion of haem to biliverdin.
Answer ▷ *K*=Spleen, bone marrow and liver.

Item 2 ▶ Conversion of biliverdin to bilirubin.
Answer ▷ *K*=Spleen, bone marrow and liver.

Item 3 ▶ Unconjugated bilirubin complexed with albumin.
Answer ▷ *B*=Circulation.

Item 4 ▶ Conjugation of bilirubin with glucuronic acid.
Answer ▷ *G*=Liver.

Item 5 ▶ Conversion of conjugated bilirubin to stercobilin.
Answer ▷ *D*=Gastrointestinal tract distal to the entry of the common bile duct.

Commentary

Purpose

The purpose of this EMQ is to test your understanding of some aspects of the metabolism of bilirubin.

Content

The lead-in statement is short and precise. The list of options contains 12 different options representing different parts of the human body.

Answers

Item 1=*K* ▶ Conversion of haem to biliverdin takes place within the cells of the reticuloendothelial system; spleen, bone marrow and liver. Haem is converted to biliverdin and the reaction is catalysed by the enzyme haem-oxygenase.

Item 2=*K* ▶ Again biliverdin is converted to bilirubin within the cells of the reticuloendothelial system and the reaction is catalysed by the enzyme biliverdin reductase.

Item 3=*B* ▶ Unconjugated bilirubin is complexed with albumin in circulating blood. This is a mechanism whereby bilirubin is transported from the spleen and bone marrow to the liver.

Item 4=*G* ▶ Bilirubin is conjugated with glucuronic acid in the liver.

Item 5=*D* ▶ Conjugated bilirubin is converted to stercobilin in the gastrointestinal tract, distal to the entry to the common bile duct.

Minimising risks and maximising your score

A candidate with a sound knowledge of the metabolism of bilirubin would be able to answer this EMQ easily. A common mistake is to memorise the various pathways including the enzymes but then disregarding a consideration of the anatomic sites where the reactions take place. At what point does bilirubin leave the reticuloendothelial system for subsequent transport to the liver? Where are the enzymes haem-oxygenase and biliverdin reductase located? What happens to bilirubin once it enters the liver? This EMQ tests a candidate's understanding of basic physiology and biochemistry.

OPTION LIST 4

Theme ▶ Understanding cell function

Domain ▶ Renal hormones

Options

	Site of biosynthesis in the kidney	Action
A	Cells of the proximal renal tubule	Inhibition of calcium absorption from the gut
B	Cells of the proximal renal tubule	Initiation of multiple signalling pathways in erythrocyte precursors
C	Cells of the proximal renal tubule	Protease which uses angiotensin 1 as its substrate
D	Cells of the proximal renal tubule	Stimulation of calcium absorption from the gut
E	Juxtaglomerular apparatus	Protease which uses angiotensin 1 as its substrate
F	Juxtaglomerular apparatus	Protease which uses angiotensinogen as its substrate

	Site of biosynthesis in the kidney	Action
G	Juxtaglomerular apparatus	Protease which uses haemoglobin as its substrate
H	Juxtaglomerular apparatus	Stimulation of calcium absorption from the gut
I	Renal peritubular endothelial cells	Initiation of multiple signalling pathways in erythrocyte precursors
J	Renal peritubular endothelial cells	Initiation of multiple signalling pathways in erythrocytes
K	Renal peritubular endothelial cells	Initiation of multiple signalling pathways in hepatocytes
L	Renal peritubular endothelial cells	Stimulation of iron absorption from the gut

Instructions

The list of options gives descriptions of the renal sites of biosynthesis and actions of different molecules. Select the **single** correct profile for each of the substances in the items below. Each option may be used once, more than once or not at all.

Item 1 ▶ Erythropoietin.
Answer ▷ *I* = Renal peritubular endothelial cells; Initiation of multiple signalling pathways in erythrocyte precursors.

Item 2 ▶ 1α-,25 dihydroxycholecalciferol.
Answer ▷ *D* = Cells of the proximal renal tubule; Stimulation of calcium absorption from the gut.

Item 3 ▶ Renin.
Answer ▷ *F* = Juxtaglomerular apparatus; Protease which uses angiotensinogen as its substrate.

Commentary

Purpose

The purpose of this EMQ is to test a candidate's understanding of renal hormones, exactly where they are produced and their actions.

Content

The lead-in statement is short and precise. There are 12 options and each one of them describes a different site of production within the kidney and a metabolic action.

Answer

Item 1 = I ▶ erythropoietin is produced in the renal peritubular endothelial cells and it stimulates erythropoiesis by initiating the formation of copious amounts of relevant mRNA in erythrocyte precursors.

Item 2 = D ▶ 1α,-25 dihydroxycholecalciferol is produced in the cells of the proximal renal tubule and its main biochemical action is to stimulate calcium absorption from the gut.

Item 3 = F ▶ renin; it is a protease which is produced in the juxtoglomerular apparatus and it converts angiotensinogen to angiotensin 1.

Minimising risk and maximising your score

This EMQ is straightforward but there are a few potential pitfalls. Familiarity with current knowledge is vital to pass the examination. Some candidates may consider the juxtaglomerular apparatus as the site of production of erythropoietin. A candidate who is not sure of the site of origin of the erythropoietin may confuse '*I*' with '*B*'. Also, a less than careful reading of the question may lead some candidates to confuse '*I*' with '*J*'. Erythropoietin initiates multiple signalling pathways in erythrocyte precursors, not in the erythrocytes themselves. Renin converts angiotensinogen to angiotensin 1; therefore, angiotensinogen is the substrate for renin which acts as a protease. Some candidates may confuse Item '*F*' with '*E*'. Once you have selected the 'correct' option it is well worth reading it a second time to make sure that it says what you think it states.

OPTION LIST 5

Theme ▶ Understanding human structure

Domain ▶ Anatomy of the ovary

Options

	Arterial blood supply	Venous drainage	Secretion of progesterone
A	Left ovarian artery, branch of the abdominal aorta	Left ovarian vein leading to the left internal iliac vein	Mainly by the granulosa cells
B	Left ovarian artery, branch of the abdominal aorta	Left ovarian vein leading to the left renal vein	By the corpus luteum during the luteal phase
C	Left ovarian artery, branch of the left internal iliac artery	Left ovarian vein leading to the left internal iliac vein	By the corpus luteum during the follicular phase
D	Left ovarian artery, branch of the left middle rectal artery	Left ovarian vein leading to the left renal vein	By the corpus luteum after fertilisation
E	Right ovarian artery, branch of the abdominal aorta	Right ovarian vein leading to the inferior vena cava	By the corpus luteum during the luteal phase
F	Right ovarian artery, branch of the abdominal aorta	Right ovarian vein leading to the inferior vena cava	Mainly by the granulosa cells

	Arterial blood supply	Venous drainage	Secretion of progesterone
G	Right ovarian artery, branch of the right internal iliac artery	Right ovarian vein leading to the inferior vena cava	By the corpus luteum during the follicular phase
H	Right ovarian artery, branch of the right middle rectal artery	Right ovarian vein leading to the right internal iliac vein	By the corpus luteum after fertilisation

Instructions

The list of options shows different profiles of an organ. Choose the **single** correct description in terms of blood supply and secretion of progesterone for each of the items below. Each option may be used once, more than once or not at all.

Item 1 ▶ Right ovary.
Answer ▷ *E*=Right ovarian artery, branch of the abdominal aorta; Right ovarian vein leading to the inferior vena cava; By the corpus luteum during the luteal phase.

Item 2 ▶ Left ovary.
Answer ▷ *B*=Left ovarian artery, branch of the abdominal aorta; Left ovarian vein leading to the left renal vein; By the corpus luteum during the luteal phase.

Commentary

Purpose

The purpose of this EMQ is to test your knowledge of basic pelvic anatomy.

Content

The lead-in statement explains that the candidate must choose the correct description of blood supply for each of the organs referred to in the items. The question also tests a candidate's knowledge of when progesterone is selected by the ovary and from which structure the hormone comes from.

Answer

Item 1 = E ▶ The right ovary receives its blood supply from the right ovarian artery which is a branch of the abdominal aorta. Its venous drainage is through the right ovarian vein which leads to the inferior vena cava. The corpus luteum secretes progesterone during the luteal phase.

Item 2 = B ▶ One key difference between the venous drainage of the right and left ovaries is that the left ovarian vein leads to the left renal vein in most women. Again, the corpus luteum secretes progesterone during the luteal phase.

Minimising risk and maximising your score

This is an example of a very easy EMQ. One possible pitfall is that the candidate would try and read through the long list of options with its complex appearance. Many of the options appear to be misleading. Does the corpus luteum secrete progesterone after fertilisation? Indeed it does. However, options which contain that particular statement do not incorporate the correct answers for arterial blood supply and venous drainage of the ovary. A candidate who is familiar with the blood supply to the ovary and who knows that the corpus luteum secretes progesterone during the luteal phase would select the correct answers within seconds. This particular question also serves to underline the need for practising EMQs before the examination.

OPTION LIST 6

Theme ▶ Understanding cell function

Domain ▶ Membrane transport systems

Options

A Antiport
B Carrier-mediated diffusion
C Simple diffusion
D Solvent drag
E Symport
F Voltage-gated ion channel

Instructions

A research team has discovered different types of new molecules and is studying their transport across plasma membranes. Some experimental data are provided in the items below. The list of options contains different types of membrane transport. Select the most appropriate option for each item. Each option may be used once, more than once or not at all.

Item 1 ▶ The molecules appear to move across the membrane from high to low concentration at a maximum rate of 1000 per second. Inhibition of Na^+, K^+ – ATPase has no effect on transport.
Answer ▷ *B* = Carrier-mediated diffusion.

Item 2 ▶ The molecules are transported across the membrane against their electrochemical gradient. Molecules with a similar structure do not cross the membrane at all. However, the research team notes that sodium Na^+ ions are transported in the opposite direction to the molecules under study. Inhibition of Na^+, K^+ – ATPase stops transport.
Answer ▷ *A* = Antiport.

Commentary

Purpose

This EMQ tests a candidate's understanding of membrane transport system.

Content

The lead-in statement describes how a research team has discovered different types of new molecules and studied their transport across plasma membranes. The data provided in the items should be used by the candidate to deduce the type of membrane transport system in each study. The candidate must then select the most appropriate option for each item from the list of options.

Answers

In order to obtain full marks for this particular EMQ the candidate must understand different types of membrane transport systems. Briefly, the different types of membrane transport systems are as follows:

- solvent drag
- passive diffusion (simple diffusion)
- channel-mediated diffusion
- carrier-mediated diffusion (uniport)
- ATP-mediated diffusion
- symport
- antiport.

ATP-mediated diffusion, symport and antiport systems require energy. Passive diffusion, channel-mediated diffusion and uniport carrier-mediated diffusion function on concentration and electrochemical gradients. The different types of membrane transport systems can also be classified further depending on substrate specificity, inhibition by sodium potassium ATPase inhibitors, saturation kinetics and whether or not there is a co-transported ion or molecule and what direction that particular co-transported ion or molecule moves in. A candidate who has a sound understanding of these principles would find the answers to both items quite straightforward.

Item 1 = B ▶ Carrier-mediated diffusion.

Item 2 = A ▶ Antiport.

Minimising risk and maximising your score

This EMQ illustrates how the examination will test the candidate's understanding of concepts. The style of questioning is not one which demands a true/false answer. A candidate is asked to interpret experimental data.

In Item 1, the molecules appear to move across the membrane across their concentration gradient. The process is not dependent upon energy, as inhibition of sodium potassium ATPase has no effect on transport. What is the relevance of the maximum rate of 1000 molecules per second? This particular rate of transport would distinguish carrier-mediated diffusion from channel-mediated diffusion, where the rate of transport of molecules would be in the order of 10,000,000 molecules or ions per second. In fact, the option of channel-mediated diffusion is not even offered as an option. Here, the examiners are being helpful.

In Item 2, it is obvious that energy is being expended as (a) the molecules are transported across the membrane against their electrochemical gradient and (b) inhibition of sodium potassium ATPase stops transport. Molecules with a similar structure do not cross the membrane at all, indicating substrate specificity. Sodium ions are transported in the opposite direction to the molecules under study; an example of an active antiport system.

OPTION LIST 7

Theme ▶ Understanding cell function

Domain ▶ Physiology, intercellular signal transduction 1

Options

A Autocrine
B Endocrine
C Juxtacrine
D Paracrine
E Synaptic

Instructions

A research team is investigating different methods of intercellular signal transduction. Their findings regarding different molecules that act as signals are provided in the items below. Select the method of signalling for each of the items below from the list of options. Each option may be used once, more than once or not at all.

Item 1 ▶ The molecule has a low molecular weight and is directly transferred from the cell which produces it to the nearby target cell. Further study shows that the molecule travels across the membrane of the target cell through channel-mediated diffusion.
Answer ▷ *C* = Juxtacrine.

Item 2 ▶ The molecule is produced and packaged in a glandular cell. It is secreted in response to a specific stimulus. The research team discovers that the molecule is transported in the circulation to a target cell in another part of the body. The molecule binds to a specific receptor when it reaches the target cell. Molecules with a very similar structure are unable to bind to the same receptor.
Answer ▷ *B* = Endocrine.

Item 3 ▶ The molecule is a short-chain polypeptide and is released by the cell which produces it into the extracellular space. The molecule passively diffuses to its target cell and the initial concentration around the target cell is measurable in millimoles. The molecule binds to a receptor on the cell membrane of the target cell. Once the concentration of the molecule falls, rapid dissociation from the receptor is observed.
Answer ▷ *D* = Paracrine.

Item 4 ▶ The molecule is a very large polypeptide which is produced by a cell in response to inflammation. The molecule binds to a receptor on the same cell.
Answer ▷ *A* = Autocrine.

Commentary

Purpose

This EMQ is designed to test a candidate's understanding of intercellular signal transduction systems and the application of basic knowledge to interpret scientific findings.

Content

The lead-in statement states clearly that a research team has been investigating different methods of inter-cellular signal transduction and that their findings regarding different molecules are provided in the items of the EMQ. The candidate is asked to read through the items, interpret the findings, and select the correct method of signalling from the list of options. The list of options is suitably short.

Answers

The various different methods of intercellular signal transduction can be distinguished on the basis of several factors which include:

- the distance between the site of production of a molecular signal and its target cell
- the molecular weight of the signalling substance
- the type of receptor on the target cell
- the method of transport from site of production to the target cell
- the concentration of the signalling agent in the region of the target cell
- the affinity of the signalling agent to the receptor on the target cell.

If the molecule has a low molecular weight and there is direct transfer from the cell which produces it to the juxtapositioned target cell with diffusion across the membrane of the target cell, then that is an example of a juxtacrine system. If a molecule (signalling agent) is produced and packaged in a cell which is some distance away from the target cell, the signalling agent is released in response to a specific stimulus, transported in the circulation (usually bound to a transport protein) to a target cell in another part of body with high affinity binding to a specific receptor on the target cell, then that is an example of an endocrine system. The concentration of the signalling agent in the blood is usually very low – measured in picomoles or nanomoles. Once the molecule has bound to its specific receptor on the target cell (with great affinity) dissociation is difficult to achieve. In a paracrine system, the molecules which act as signalling agents can be diverse and can include proteins, small peptides and simple organic molecules, such as histamine and adenosine. In a paracrine system, the molecule diffuses passively to its target cell which is nearby but not necessarily juxtapositioned and the initial concentration around the target cell is measurable in millimoles. The molecule binds to a receptor in the cell membrane of the target cell but substrate specificity is comparatively low. In an autocrine system, the molecule which acts as a signalling agent tends to be very large and is produced by a cell in response to a specific stimulus, such as inflammation. The molecule then binds to a receptor on the same cell. Autocrine signalling is often observed in embryonic systems. Therefore the answers are as follows:

Item 1 ▶ C = Juxtacrine.

Item 2 ▶ B = Endocrine.

Item 3 ▶ D = Paracrine.

Item 4 ▶ A = Autocrine.

Minimising the risk and maximising your score

This EMQ demands a thorough understanding of mechanisms of intercellular signal transduction. The candidate must also demonstrate an ability to interpret basic scientific data as presented in the items. There is no substitute for reading a good textbook.

OPTION LIST 8

Theme ▶ Pharmacology

Domain ▶ Antimicrobials 1

Options

A Amoebicidal in plasma
B Blockage of protein kinase receptors
C Enhancement of photosensitivity
D Enhancement of radiosensitivity
E Increased biliary excretion
F Inhibition of bacterial cell wall synthesis
G Inhibition of bacterial nucleic acid synthesis
H Inhibition of bacterial protein synthesis
I Inhibition of retroviral fusion
J Inhibition of retroviral non-nucleoside reverse transcriptase
K Inhibition of retroviral nucleoside reverse transcriptase
L Inhibition of retroviral protease
M Initiation of an anaphylactic reaction
N Lysis of bacterial cell wall
O Production of beta lactamase
P Schizonticidal within erythrocytes
Q Schizonticidal within hepatocytes

Instructions

The list of options contains different pharmacological reactions. Select the reaction which describes the principal antimicrobial activity of the drugs in the items below. Each option may be used once, more than once or not at all.

Item 1 ▶ Methicillin.
Answer ▷ *F*=Inhibition of bacterial cell wall synthesis.

Item 2 ▶ Vancomycin.
Answer ▷ *F*=Inhibition of bacterial cell wall synthesis.

Item 3 ▶ Cefuroxime.
Answer ▷ *F*=Inhibition of bacterial cell wall synthesis.

Item 4 ▶ Gentamicin.
Answer ▷ *H*=Inhibition of bacterial protein synthesis.

Item 5 ▶ Nalidixic acid.
Answer ▷ *G*=Inhibition of bacterial nucleic acid synthesis.

Item 6 ▶ Primaquine.
Answer ▷ *Q*=Schizonticidal within hepatocytes.

Item 7 ▶ Pyrimethamine.
Answer ▷ *P*=Schizonticidal within erythrocytes.

Item 8 ▶ Nevirapine.
Answer ▷ *J*=Inhibition of retroviral non-nucleoside reverse transcriptase.

Commentary

Purpose

The aim of this EMQ is to test a candidate's knowledge of antimicrobial activity.

Content

The lead-in statement is concise and unambiguous. Each of the items refers to a certain antibiotic and the candidate has to choose its principle antimicrobial activity from the list of 17 options. This is an example of an EMQ which demonstrates the need for an adequate level of knowledge and also demonstrates a long list of options.

Answers

Item 1=F ▶ Inhibition of bacterial cell wall synthesis.

Item 2 = *F* ▶ Inhibition of bacterial cell wall synthesis.

Item 3 = *F* ▶ Inhibition of bacterial cell wall synthesis.

Item 4 = *H* ▶ Inhibition of bacterial protein synthesis.

Item 5 = *G* ▶ Inhibition of bacterial nucleic acid synthesis.

Item 6 = *Q* ▶ Schizonticidal within hepatocytes.

Item 7 = *P* ▶ Schizonticidal within erythrocytes.

Item 8 = *J* ▶ Inhibition of retroviral non-nucleoside reverse transcriptase.

Minimising the risk and maximising your score

A sound knowledge of drugs and their actions fulfils one of the core requirements of 'understanding measurement and manipulation'. The well-prepared candidate would be able to demonstrate knowledge of antimicrobial activity of specific drugs and be prepared to answer further questions on the exact mechanisms of action. A variation on the theme of this particular EMQ may be: 'Select the exact site within the cell where a certain antibiotic will bind'. The list of options would then consist of different intracellular sites.

There are several functional distracters in option list 8 and they are best ignored.

4 | Full mock examination paper I (paper I type)

EMQ SECTION

OPTIONS

A	Cerebellum	E	Parietal lobe
B	Frontal lobe	F	Pons
C	Hypothalamus	G	Temporal lobe
D	Occipital lobe	H	Thalamus

Instructions

The list of options contains different parts of the human central nervous system. Select the **single** correct site of each of the structures in the items below from the list of options. Each option may be used once, more than once or not at all.

Question 1 ▷ Primary motor cortex.

Question 2 ▷ Primary somatosensory cortex.

OPTIONS

A	1 cm	F	10 cm
B	2 cm	G	15 cm
C	4 cm	H	25 cm
D	5 cm	I	35 cm
E	8 cm	J	40 cm

Instructions

The items below refer to anatomic structures or dimensions in the adult female. Select the **single** best matching length of each structure or dimension from the list of options. Each option may be used once, more than once or not at all.

Question 3 ▷ Right ureter.

Question 4 ▷ Right common iliac artery.

OPTIONS

A Day 1
B Day 2
C Day 3
D Day 4
E Day 5
F Day 7
G Day 8
H Day 9
I Day 13
J Day 15
K Day 18
L Day 20
M Day 22
N Day 28
O Day 35
P Day 36
Q Day 44
R Day 49
S Day 56
T Day 57

Instructions

The list of options contains references to timing with the pronuclear stage following fertilisation at Day '0'. The items refer to stages in early human development. Select the **single** most correct timing of each stage from the list of options. Each option may be used once, more than once or not at all.

Question 5 ▷ Eight-cell stage.

Question 6 ▷ Development of the definitive yolk sac.

OPTIONS

	Target	Hormone
A	Adrenal medulla	Aldosterone
B	Cells of the renal proximal tubule	1α, 25-dihydroxycholecalciferol (calcitriol)

	Target	Hormone
C	Corpus luteum of the ovary	Progesterone
D	Endometrium	Progesterone
E	Follicular cells of the ovary	Estradiol
F	Hepatocytes	1α, 25-dihydroxycholecalciferol (calcitriol)
G	Renal juxtaglomerular cells	Angiotensin I
H	Salivary glands	Epidermal growth factor
I	Zona fasciculata of the adrenal gland	Cortisol
J	Zona glomerulosa of the adrenal gland	Aldosterone

Instructions

Select the **single** option which describes the correct target organ or tissue and the steroid hormone the target produces for each of the substances referred to in the items below. Each option may be used once, more than once or not at all.

Question 7 ▷ Adrenocorticotrophic hormone.

Question 8 ▷ Luteinising hormone.

OPTIONS

	Site of biosynthesis	Effect on serum calcium
A	Adrenal cortex	Lowered
B	Liver	No effect
C	Liver	Lowered
D	Parathyroid gland (chief cells)	Elevated
E	Parathyroid gland (chief cells)	No effect
F	Parathyroid gland (chief cells)	Lowered

	Site of biosynthesis	Effect on serum calcium
G	Thyroid gland (follicular cells)	No effect
H	Thyroid gland (follicular cells)	Lowered
I	Thyroid gland (parafollicular C cells)	Elevated
J	Thyroid gland (parafollicular C cells)	Lowered

Instructions

Select the **single** most appropriate profile for the hormones in the items below. Each option may be used once, more than once or not at all.

Question 9 ▷ Calcitonin.

Question 10 ▷ Parathormone.

OPTIONS

	Type of nucleic acid in viral genome	Mode of infection of the baby
A	DNA	Transplacental
B	DNA	Perinatal
C	DNA	No risk of infection
D	RNA	Transplacental
E	RNA	Perinatal
F	RNA	No risk of infection

Instructions

The list of options describes the type of nucleic acid in a virus and the mode of infection if any of the baby by that virus. Select the **single** correct option for the virus in the item below.

Question 11 ▷ Parvovirus B 19.

OPTIONS

A *Borrelia burgdoferi*
B *Borrelia recurrentis*
C *Chlamydia pneumoniae*
D *Chlamydia psittaci*
E *Chlamydia trachomatis*
F *Haemophilus ducreyi*
G *Haemophilus haemolyticus*
H *Haemophilus parahaemolyticus*
I *Haemophilus paraphrophilus*
J *Mycobacterium leprae*
K *Mycobacterium tuberculosis*
L *Plasmodium falciparum*
M *Plasmodium vivax*
N *Treponema carateum*
O *Treponema pallidum* subspecies endemicum
P *Treponema pallidum* subspecies pallidum
Q *Treponema pallidum* subspecies pertenue
R *Trypanosoma brucei* gambiense
S *Trypanosoma cruzi*
T *Yersinia pestis*

Instructions

Select the **single** aetiological agent from the list of options for each of the human diseases listed in the items below. Each option may be used once, more than once or not at all.

Question 12 ▷ Primary syphilis.

Question 13 ▷ Lyme disease.

OPTIONS

	Mechanism of action	Site of action
A	Carbonic anhydrase inhibitor	Collecting tubule

	Mechanism of action	Site of action
B	Carbonic anhydrase inhibitor	Proximal tubule
C	Inhibitor of potassium transport	Juxtaglomerular apparatus
D	Inhibitor of renal epithelial sodium channels	Collecting duct only
E	Inhibitor of renal epithelial sodium channels	Late portion of the distal tubule and the collecting duct
F	Inhibitor of sodium and chloride ion transport	Distal convoluted tubule
G	Inhibitor of sodium and chloride ion transport	Proximal tubule
H	Inhibitor of sodium, potassium and chloride ion transport	Thick portion of the ascending limb
I	Inhibitor of sodium, potassium and lithium ion transport	Distal convoluted tubule
J	Mineralocorticoid receptor antagonist	Juxtaglomerular apparatus
K	Mineralocorticoid receptor antagonist	Late portion of the distal tubule and the collecting duct
L	Osmotic	Distal convoluted tubule only
M	Osmotic	Juxtaglomerular apparatus
N	Osmotic	Loop of Henle

Instructions

The list of options refers to the mechanism of action and site of action within the kidney of various drugs. Select the **single** correct mechanism and site of action for each of the diuretics in the items listed below from the list of options. Each option may be used once, more than once or not at all.

Question 14 ▷ Acetazolamide.

Question 15 ▷ Mannitol.

OPTIONS

A Altered distribution
B Decreased absorption
C Increased urinary excretion
D Induction of a new mutation in cytochrome P450 genes
E Induction of cytochrome P450
F Inhibition of cytochrome P450
G Production of antibodies against specific drug receptor
H Underlying genetic polymorphism of cytochrome P450 genes

Instructions

The list of options refers to different factors which may affect drug metabolism. The item below refers to an example of drug metabolism. Select the **single** most likely mechanism for the item.

Question 16 ▷ An otherwise healthy woman was using the combined oral contraceptive pill and was given a course of ampicillin tablets for suspected urinary tract infection. The woman developed diarrhoea and a few days alter she experienced irregular vaginal bleeding.

OPTIONS

A 0.2
B 0.67
C 1
D 10
E 20
F 45
G 100
H 120

Instructions

A screening test for chlamydial infection of the cervix based on the clinical appearance of the cervix was carried out on *N* women. The results of the screening test were compared with a gold standard test for chlamydial infection of the cervix. The results of the study are presented in the table below:

	Disease present	Disease absent
Screen positive	w	y
Screen negative	x	z

The item below provides different values for N, w, x, y and z. Calculate the approximate likelihood ratio for each study and select the **single** correct answer from the list of options.

Question 17 ▷ $N = 200$, $w = 50$, $x = 50$, $y = 50$, $z = 50$.

OPTIONS

A	6	H	300
B	25	I	400
C	26	J	500
D	50	K	1000
E	61	L	2000
F	100	M	2500
G	250	N	1000

Instructions

A large -scale study was carried out to assess the benefits of a new drug which would prevent fractured neck of the femur due to osteoporosis in post-menopausal women. The study was carried out correctly using a treatment group and an appropriate control group. The number of women who sustained a fractured neck of femur due to osteoporosis was measured reliably in each group and the results are given in the table below:

Group	Women with fractured neck of femur (n)	Women without fractured neck of femur (n)
Control	N_1	N_3
Study	N_2	N_4

The items below provide different values for $N1$, $N2$, $N3$ and $N4$. Calculate the number of women who need to receive the new drug in order to prevent one new fracture of the femoral neck due to postmenopausal osteoporosis for the item below and select the **single** correct answer from the list of options.

Question 18 ▷ $N1 = 50$; $N2 = 25$; $N3 = 9950$; $N4 = 9975$.

OPTIONS

A 2 mmHg
B 3 mmHg
C 4 mmHg
D 5 mmHg
E 6 mmHg
F 7 mmHg
G 8 mmHg
H 9 mmHg
I 10 mmHg
J 16 mmHg
K 25 mmHg
L 30 mmHg
M 31 mmHg
N 32 mmHg

Instructions

For each of the studies below, calculate and select the **single** correct standard deviation from the list of options. Each of the studies refers to systolic blood pressure in normal healthy pregnant women, the measurements of systolic blood pressure show a perfect Gaussian distribution and N = the number of women in each study. Each option may be used once, more than once or not at all.

Question 19 ▷ N = 5000; mean = 100 mmHg; variance = 9.

Question 20 ▷ N = 500, mean = 110 mmHg, variance = 16.

All question items 21–68, *A* to *E* inclusive, to be answered TRUE or FALSE.

Question 21 ▷ The vulva comprises the following:

A Bartholin's gland.
B labium majus.
C labia minora.
D anus.
E clitoris.

Question 22 ▷ The arterial blood supply to the vulva includes the

A deep circumflex iliac artery.
B median sacral artery.
C superficial external pudendal artery.
D deep external pudendal artery.
E internal pudendal artery.

Question 23 ▷ The diaphragm

A receives its motor nerve supply from the lower six intercostal nerves.
B has a concave upper surface.
C has an aortic aperture at the level of the eighth thoracic vertebra.
D is capable of lending additional power to all expulsive efforts.
E is continuous with the outer layer of the muscle of the oesophagus.

Question 24 ▷ The vagina receives arterial blood supply from the following branches of the internal iliac artery:

A vaginal.
B superior vesical.
C uterine.
D obturator.
E internal pudendal.

Question 25 ▷ The following are branches of the abdominal aorta:

A uterine artery.
B femoral artery.
C inferior phrenic artery.
D median sacral artery.
E coeliac trunk.

Question 26 ▷ The anal canal

A is approximately 5 cm long in the adult.
B is lined by columnar epithelium along its whole length.
C is lined by keratinised stratified squamous epithelium along its lower half.
D is supplied by the median sacral arteries.
E contains the valves of Houston.

Question 27 ▷ The vagina

A is innervated by the pelvic splanchnic nerves.
B has on outer circular layer of muscle.
C has an inner longitudinal layer of muscle.
D is surrounded by skeletal muscle in its lower part.
E has a posterior wall which is covered by peritonum over its upper (and internal) quarter.

Question 28 ▷ The uterus

A weighs approximately 200 grams in a healthy non-pregnant adult woman.
B weighs approximately 1 kg (without contents) at 40 weeks of gestation in a healthy pregnancy.
C contains lymph vessels which diminish significantly in size during a normal pregnancy.
D receives its main blood supply from the uterine artery.
E is drained partly by the lateral aortic nodes.

Question 29 ▷ The pelvic ureter

A lies in extraperitoneal areolar tissue.

B descends on the pelvic side wall along the anterior border of the greater sciatic notch.

C lies inferior to the uterine artery and superior to the lateral vaginal fornix.

D lies superior to both the uterine vein and the lateral vaginal fornix.

E lies lateral to the inferior vesical artery and is 2 cm lateral to the internal cervical os at the level of the vaginal fornix.

Question 30 ▷ The uterine artery

A is a branch of the anterior division of the internal iliac artery.

B gives rise to an ascending branch which anastomoses with the tubal branch of the ovarian artery.

C gives rise to a descending branch which supplies the rectum.

D is separated from the uterine vein by the ureter.

E carries deoxygenated maternal blood during pregnancy.

Question 31 ▷ The paramesonephric ducts

A lie lateral to the mesonephric ducts over most of their lengths at the time of their formation.

B begin to form at 6 weeks.

C begin to form before the mesonephric ducts.

D contain germ cells.

E give rise to the lower third of the ureter.

Question 32 ▷ The endoderm epithelium gives rise to the following:

A hepatocytes.

B epithelial lining of the vesical trigone.

C β-cells of the islets of Langerhans.

D peritoneum of greater omentum.

E peritoneum of lesser omentum.

Question 33 ▷ The embryonic mesenchyme gives rise to the following:
A myometrium.
B pharyngeal glands.
C hepatocytes.
D cerebellum.
E basophils.

Question 34 ▷ The surface ectoderm epithelium gives rise to the following:
A epithelium of the cornea.
B pubic hair.
C lining of the urinary bladder.
D epithelial lining of the vesical trigone.
E cerebellum.

Question 35 ▷ The neural crest gives rise to the following:
A melanocytes.
B odontoblasts.
C hypodermis of face.
D dermis of face.
E pia mater.

Question 36 ▷ The adrenal cortex is the site of biosynthesis of
A cortisol.
B adrenaline.
C vasopressin.
D dehydroepiandrosterone.
E aldosterone.

Question 37 ▷ Adrenocorticotrophic hormone (ACTH)
A is secreted by the anterior lobe of the pituitary gland.
B is secreted in response to corticotrophin-releasing hormone.
C exerts its major action on the cells of the adrenal medulla.
D activates melanocyte-stimulating hormone receptors.
E is composed of two subunits.

Question 38 ▷ Growth hormone

A stimulates the biosynthesis of insulin-like growth factors in the liver.

B inhibits the biosynthesis of insulin-like growth factors in the chondrocytes.

C inhibits the biosynthesis of insulin-like growth factors in muscle.

D stimulates lipolysis.

E inhibits gluconeogenesis in muscle.

Question 39 ▷ Follicle-stimulating hormone

A is a glycoprotein.

B has a molecular weight of 30,000.

C is secreted by the anterior lobe of the pituitary gland.

D stimulates the seminiferous tubules in the male.

E is antagonised by insulin.

Question 40 ▷ Thyroid-stimulating hormone

A is a lipoprotein.

B contains 20,000 amino acids.

C binds to a specific receptor on the basal membrane of epithelial cells of the thyroid gland.

D stimulates the biosynthesis of thyroid hormones T3 and T4.

E stimulates the release of thyroid hormones T3 and T4.

Question 41 ▷ The following substances are released from the hypothalamus:

A gonadotrophin-releasing hormone (GnRH).

B thyrotropin-releasing hormone (TRH).

C corticotrophin-like intermediary peptide (CLIP).

D angiotensinogen.

E follicle-stimulating hormone (FSH).

Question 42 ▷ The pancreas secretes the following:

A gastrin G-34.

B trypsin.

C carboxypolypeptidase.

D intrinsic factor.

E renin.

Question 43 ▷ Insulin

A is produced in the β-cells of the islets of Langerhans in the pancreas.

B is composed of two amino acid chains.

C has a plasma half-life that is approximately 6 minutes.

D is degraded mainly by the kidney.

E activity is enhanced by insulinase.

Question 44 ▷ Insulin secretion is increased by

A glucagon.

B cortisol.

C growth hormone.

D sulphonylureas.

E stimulation of α-adrenergic receptors by noradrenaline.

Question 45 ▷ Aldosterone

A is synthesised in the cells of the adrenal medulla.

B binds to receptors on the cells of the distal tubule of the kidney.

C enhances the renal tubular reabsorption of sodium (Na^+).

D increases the urinary excretion of potassium (K^+).

E enhances the renal tubular reabsorption of hydrogen (H^+).

Question 46 ▷ The following infections are paired correctly with the causal organism:

A Syphilis : *Haemophilus ducrei.*
B Lymphogranuloma venereum : *Mycobacterium tuberculosis.*
C Gonorrhoea : *Trichomonas vaginalis.*
D Malaria : *Plasmodium vivax.*
E Scabies : *Herpes simplex* virus.

Question 47 ▷ *Candida albicans*

A is a dimorphic fungus.
B forms hyphae when invasive.
C is the cause of histoplasmosis.
D is sensitive to broad-spectrum antibiotics.
E is a cause of chorioamnionitis.

Question 48 ▷ *Giardia lambia*

A may infect the pregnant woman.
B has specific molecules for attachment to the microvilli of epithelial cells.
C has a microvillar sucking disc.
D may cause severe diarrhoea.
E is sensitive to metronidazole.

Question 49 ▷ Gonorrhoea is a cause of

A urethritis in women.
B urethritis in men.
C systemic lupus erythematosus.
D chancres.
E condyloma accuminatum.

Question 50 ▷ Bacteria may acquire virulence by

A transduction.
B reduced penicillin binding.
C plasmid transfer which enables production of protease against immunoglobulin A (IgA).

D plasmid transfer which enables production of lipopolysaccharide in the cell wall.
E insertion of a transposon which enables coating with fibronectin.

Question 51 ▷ Viruses
A contain either DNA or RNA.
B do not possess a cell wall.
C can only replicate in living cells.
D do not possess mitochondria.
E possess ribosomes.

Question 52 ▷ The following organisms are part of the normal flora in the stomach:
A lactobacilli.
B *Escherichia coli.*
C enterobacteria.
D *Vibrio cholerae.*
E *Taenia solium.*

Question 53 ▷ The following drugs are likely to lower the serum glucose:
A β-adrenergic receptor antagonists.
B salicylates.
C bromocriptine.
D adrenaline.
E insulin.

Question 54 ▷ The following are examples of penicillins:
A imipenem.
B aztreonam.
C flucloxacillin.
D vancomycin.
E methicillin.

Question 55 ▷ Metformin

A is a sulphonylurea.
B lowers serum glucose.
C decreases the secretion of glucagon.
D is absorbed from the small intestine following oral intake.
E has a half-life of 2 hours.

Question 56 ▷ Lidocaine

A is an ester of benzoic acid.
B is absorbed through intact skin.
C is dealkylated in the liver.
D must always be administered with a vasoconstrictor.
E may lead to coma if used in excess.

Question 57 ▷ The following are examples of aminoglycosides:

A penicillamine.
B gentamicin.
C streptomycin.
D actinomycin D.
E amoxicillin.

Question 58 ▷ The following antibiotics contain a ß-lactam ring:

A penicillin G.
B penicillin V.
C clindamycin.
D cephradine.
E cefuroxime.

Question 59 ▷ Trastuzumab

A is an aromatase inhibitor.
B should be taken orally.
C may be used in the adjuvant treatment of breast cancer which over-expresses human epidermal growth factor receptor 2.
D is cardiotoxic.
E is capable of inducing apoptosis.

Question 60 ▷ The two sample (unpaired) t-test

A is a non-parametric test.

B compares two independent samples from the same population.

C may be used in a study to compare maternal weight at delivery with paternal weight at delivery.

D may be used in a study to compare tumour volume before and after chemotherapy.

E is an example of a method of carrying out two-way analysis of variance by ranks.

Question 61 ▷ Regression by least squares method

A can be applied to measurements with a normal distribution.

B applies to quantitative variables.

C analyses two variables and allows one variable to be predicted from the other.

D can be used to determine whether birth weight can be predicted from maternal calorific intake.

E can be used to predict whether or not shoulder dystocia can be predicted from maternal calorific intake.

Question 62 ▷ When comparing two groups,

A the odds ratio is a method of representing probability.

B the relative risk is a summary measure of the ratio of the risk of an actual event.

C for a very rare event the odds ratio and the relative risk will be similar.

D a high *P* value is strong evidence against the null hypothesis.

E wide confidence intervals are preferable to narrow confidence intervals.

Question 63 ▷ A study was carried out of birth weight among immigrant women from South East Asia living in an inner city area. The women had uncomplicated pregnancies and the birth weights of 10,000 babies were reliably measured. The results showed a perfect Gaussian distribution with a mean birth weight of 3050 grams and a standard deviation of 150 grams. The following statements are correct:

A The median birth weight was 3050 grams.

B The mode can be calculated by subtracting variance from mean.

C Two-thirds of the babies had a birth weight between 2900 grams and 3200 grams.

D 100 babies had a birth weight in excess of 3500 grams.

E 6800 babies had a birth weight between 2900 grams and 3200 grams.

Question 64 ▷ The Kruskall Wallis test

A is an analysis of variance by ranks.

B is a non-parametric test.

C can be used in a study which examines four sets of observations on a single sample.

D assesses the strength of the association between two continuous variables.

E can be used in a study to determine whether intrauterine pressures are higher 1, 2 or 3 hours after forewater amniotomy at 40 weeks of gestation.

Question 65 ▷ The following tests may be appropriately used in studies where the variables have a skewed distribution:

A one sample (paired) t-test.

B two sample (unpaired) t-test.

C two-way analysis of variance by ranks.

D F test.

E Spearman's rank correlation coefficient.

Question 66 ▷ A study reports that the mean systolic blood pressure in a certain treatment group was 100 mmHg with a 95% confidence interval between 95 mmHg and 105 mmHg. The following conclusions are valid:

A We can be 95% confident that the true mean of that population lies between 95 mmHg and 105 mmHg.
B The interval between 95 mmHg and 105 mmHg has a 0.90 probability of containing the true population mean.
C The best estimate of the true population mean is 95 mmHg.
D The true population mean could possibly be less than 95 mmHg.
E The possibility that the true population mean is more than 110 mmHg is completely excluded.

Question 67 ▷ Evidence-based practice

A is the process of systematically finding and using contemporaneous research findings as the basis for clinical decision making.
B relies on a maximum of 50% uptake of clinical guidelines.
C requires the formulation of clear clinical questions.
D requires the critical appraisal of the validity of a research report.
E requires the measurement of performance against expected outcomes.

Question 68 ▷ The following controls are entirely appropriate when there cannot be blinding for a clinical trial:

A placebo.
B standard of care.
C historical.
D blinded evaluator.
E objective endpoint.

5 | Full mock examination paper 2 (paper 2 type)

EMQ SECTION

OPTIONS

A	10	K	5800
B	18	L	6000
C	20	M	10000
D	23	N	15000
E	100	O	17000
F	150	P	18000
G	180	Q	22000
H	1800	R	28000
I	2000	S	69000
J	5000	T	690000

Instructions

For each atom or molecule in the items below, select the molecular weight from the list of options. Each option may be used once, more than once or not at all.

Question 1 ▷ Glucose.

Question 2 ▷ Myoglobin.

OPTIONS

A α-2 antiplasmin
B Bence-Jones protein
C C-reactive protein
D Caeruloplasmin
E Cortisol-binding globulin

F Erythropoietin
G Fibrinogen
H Haptoglobin
I Myoglobin
J Plasminogen
K Prothrombin
L Sex hormone-binding globulin
M Thyroid-binding globulin
N Transferrin

Instructions

The list of options contains various different proteins in the human body. The item refers to a ligand. Select the **single** protein which binds to each ligand from the list of options.

Question 3 ▷ Iron (ferric ions).

OPTIONS

	pH	Plasma bicarbonate	Partial pressure of carbon dioxide in plasma $_{p}CO_2$
A	Decreased	Decreased	Decreased
B	Decreased	Decreased	Normal
C	Decreased	Increased	Increased
D	Decreased	Normal	Increased
E	Decreased	Normal	Normal
F	Increased	Decreased	Decreased
G	Increased	Increased	Increased
H	Increased	Increased	Normal
I	Increased	Normal	Decreased
J	Increased	Normal	Normal

Instructions

Select the **single** correct profile for the disorders of acid-base balance in the items below. Each option may be used once, more than once or not at all.

Question 4 ▷ Uncompensated metabolic acidosis.

OPTIONS

A Active antiport with hydrogen (H^+)
B Active antiport with sodium (Na^+)
C Active antiport with potassium (K^+)
D Active symport with hydrogen (H^+)
E Active symport with potassium (K^+)
F Active symport with sodium (Na^+)
G Active uniport with hydrogen (H^+)
H Active uniport with potassium (K^+)
I Active uniport with sodium (Na^+)
J Facilitated diffusion
K Passive antiport
L Passive symport
M Passive uniport
N Voltage gated ion channel

Instructions

The list of options contains different membrane transport systems. Select the **single** system which enables the transport of each of the substances in the item below.

Question 5 ▷ Sodium (Na^+) (plasma membranes of most cells).

OPTIONS

A	20–20,000 Hertz
B	20,000–30,000 Hertz
C	500,000–1,000,000 Hertz
D	1,000,000–2,000,000 Hertz
E	3,000,000–7,500,000 Hertz
F	5,000,000–10,000,000 Hertz
G	10,000,000–11,000,000 Hertz
H	5,000,000–15,000,000 Hertz

Instructions

The list of options refers to ranges of frequency of sound waves in cycles per second (1 Hertz = one cycle per second). Select the **single** correct range for the items below from the list of options. Each option may be used once, more than once or not at all.

Question 6 ▷ Audible sound.

Question 7 ▷ Diagnostic ultrasound for fetal imaging.

OPTIONS

	Probe	Target
A	Antibody	DNA
B	Antibody	Protein
C	Antibody	RNA
D	Nucleotide	DNA
E	Nucleotide	Protein
F	Nucleotide	RNA
G	Virus	DNA
H	Virus	RNA

Instructions

Select the option which shows the correct probe for a certain target in the item below.

Question 8 ▷ Southern blot

OPTIONS

	Type of inheritance	Clinical disorder
A	Autosomal dominant	Anaemia with recurrent infarction of bones, lungs and spleen
B	Autosomal dominant	Arachnodactyly, coarctation of the aorta, mitral regurgitation
C	Autosomal dominant	Neuromuscular degeneration from middle age onwards
D	Autosomal dominant	Progressive muscle weakness with onset from adulthood
E	Autosomal dominant	Ricketts
F	Autosomal dominant	Severe, chronic, transfusion-dependent anaemia
G	Autosomal recessive	Anaemia with recurrent infarction of bones, lungs and spleen
H	Autosomal recessive	Arachnodactyly, coarctation of the aorta, mitral regurgitation
I	Autosomal recessive	Hydrops fetalis and perinatal death
J	Autosomal recessive	Microcytic anaemia
K	Autosomal recessive	Neuromuscular degeneration from middle age onwards
L	Autosomal recessive	Progressive, incurable neurodegeneration in childhood
M	Autosomal recessive	Progressive muscle weakness with onset from adulthood
N	Autosomal recessive	Severe, chronic, transfusion-dependent anaemia

	Type of inheritance	Clinical disorder
O	X-linked dominant	Microcytic anaemia
P	X-linked dominant	Progressive, incurable neurodegeneration in childhood
Q	X-linked dominant	Ricketts
R	X-linked dominant	Severe bleeding from minor injuries, bleeding into joints
S	X-linked recessive	Hydrops fetalis and perinatal death
T	X-linked recessive	Increased risk of deep-vein thrombosis
U	X-linked recessive	Microcytic anaemia
V	X-linked recessive	Severe bleeding from minor injuries, bleeding into joints

Instructions

Select the option that describes the type of inheritance and salient clinical features of the single-gene disorders in the items below. Each option may be used once, more than once or not at all.

Question 9 ▷ Huntington's chorea.

Question 10 ▷ Tay-Sachs disease.

OPTIONS

A Activation of the classical pathway
B Activation of the mannose-binding ligand pathway
C Activation of the alternate pathway

Instructions

Select the **single** correct pathway of complement activation which would result from the action of the substance in the item below.

Question 11 ▷ Immunoglobulin G (IgG).

OPTIONS

A Acetic acid
B Alcian blue
C Alcian green
D Alcian red
E Aqueous iodine
F Background illumination
G Congo blue
H Congo red
I Gentian violet
J Gram stain
K Haematoxylin and eosin
L Lugol's iodine
M Martius scarlet blue
N Masson-Fontana
O Periodic Acid Schiff
P Ziehl Neelsen

Istructions

Select the **single** appropriate stain for each of the items referred to below from the list of options. Each option may be used once, more than once or not at all.

Question 12 ▷ Acidic mucin.

Question 13 ▷ Group B streptococcus.

OPTIONS

A 40
B 44
C 70
D 80
E 90
F 100
G 110
H 120
I 130
J 140
K 150
L 160
M 170
N 180
O 190
P 200

Instructions

The list of options refers to temperature in degrees Celsius. The items below refer to degrees of tissue injury. Select the **single** temperature at which the degree of tissue injury will occur from the list of options. Each option may be used once, more than once or not at all.

Question 14 ▷ Desiccation.

Question 15 ▷ Necrosis.

OPTIONS

A Acrodermatitis enteropathica
B Cardiomyopathy
C Encephalopathy
D Goitre
E Hepatic damage
F Nephropathy
G Subacute combined degeneration of the spinal cord
H Suppression of the bone marrow

Instructions

Select the **single** most likely effect of the deficiency of the trace element referred to in the item below.

Question 16 ▷ Iodine.

OPTIONS

A	5 g	I	1500 g
B	10 g	J	2300 g
C	25 g	K	3500 g
D	75 g	L	4900 g
E	200 g	M	5100 g
F	400 g	N	5500 g
G	650 g	O	5600 g
H	1100 g	P	5650 g

Instructions

The list of options contains mass in grams. Each of the items below refers to a normal human fetus in a continuing intrauterine singleton pregnancy. Select the **single** most likely fetal mass for each of the gestations in the items below. Each option may be used once, more than once or not at all.

Question 17 ▷ 12 weeks.

Question 18 ▷ 32 weeks.

innate immune response

OPTIONS

	Precursor	Function	Diapedesis	Amoeboid motion
A	Lymphoid stem cell	Production of antibodies	No	No
B	Lymphoid stem cell	Production of cytotoxins	No	No
C	Lymphoid stem cell	Production of lymph	Yes	Yes
D	Myeloblast	Formation of clots	No	No
E	Myeloblast	Phagocytosis	No	No
F	Myeloblast	Phagocytosis	Yes	Yes
G	Myeloblast	Release of heparin, histamine, bradykinin	No	Yes
H	Proerythroblast	Carriage of oxygen	No	No
I	Proerythroblast	Carriage of oxygen	Yes	No
J	Proerythroblast	Secretion of erythropoietin	No	No

Instructions

The list of options shows different profiles of a cell in terms of its function, its precursor and whether or not that cell is capable of diapedesis or amoeboid motion. Select the **single** most appropriate option for each of the cells in the items below. Each option may be used once, more than once or not at all.

Question 19 ▷ Polymorphonuclear neutrophil.

Question 20 ▷ Erythrocyte.

All question items 21–68, *A* to *E* inclusive, to be answered TRUE or FALSE.

Question 21 ▷ Erythropoietin
A is a polypeptide.
B initiates the synthesis of haemoglobin.
C is structurally related to erythromycin.
D may be isolated from the antrum of the stomach.
E is detectable in serum following bilateral nephrectomy.

Question 22 ▷ Ribosomal RNA
A constitutes 60% of the ribosome.
B is synthesised in the nucleus.
C collects in the nucleolus.
D is absent in prokaryotic cells.
E is the catalytic component of the ribosome.

Question 23 ▷ The sodium–potassium pump
A is an example of passive transport.
B transports potassium out of the cell under physiological conditions.
C requires adenosine triphosphate (ATP).
D is unique to nerve cells.
E is based around a carrier protein in the cell membrane.

Question 24 ▷ Oxytocin
A is produced in the posterior lobe of the pituitary gland.
B is derived from the precursor for antidiuretic hormone.
C stimulates testosterone synthesis in the male.
D is released with neurophysin II as part of the suckling response in lactating females.
E binds to receptors on the myometrium.

Question 25 ▷ Nitric oxide mediates the following physiological functions:

A neurotransmission in the central nervous system.
B antibacterial activity of neutrophils.
C antiprotozoal activity of macrophages.
D platelet adhesiveness.
E contraction of cardiac muscle.

Question 26 ▷ The following hormones contain a cystine disulphide bridge:

A antidiuretic hormone.
B oxytocin.
C growth hormone.
D aldosterone.
E testosterone.

Question 27 ▷ Human placental lactogen

A is composed of 2 subunits: α and β.
B stimulates lipolysis in adipose tissue.
C is produced by the breasts.
D is present at a much higher concentration in maternal blood than in the amniotic fluid.
E enhances the transfer of amino acids across the placenta to the fetus.

Question 28 ▷ The following molecules contain iron:

A bilirubin.
B biliverdin.
C deoxygenated fetal haemoglobin.
D haemoglobin S.
E urobilinogen.

Question 29 ▷ RNA polymerase

A is template-dependent.
B requires a primer.
C binds to DNA promoter.
D promotes the formation of mRNA without unwinding DNA.
E is inhibited by rifampicin in mycobacterium tuberculosis.

Question 30 ▷ Simple diffusion of a lipophilic solute across a plasma membrane

A is affected by its diffusion coefficient.
B is unaffected by its concentration gradient.
C is energy-dependent.
D can be stopped by inhibition of Na^+, K^+ – ATPase.
E requires the simultaneous transport of a molecule of similar structure to travel in the opposite direction through the same channel.

Question 31 ▷ The Golgi complex is associated with the following functions:

A synthesis of DNA.
B synthesis of RNA.
C synthesis of new membranes.
D formation of lysosomes.
E formation of peroxisomes.

Question 32 ▷ The resting membrane potential of nerve cells is

A approximately + 90 millivolts.
B determined mainly by the sodium–potassium membrane pump.
C affected by the permeability of the nerve cell membrane to sodium ions.
D affected by the diffusion of potassium ions.
E a prerequisite for the transmission of impulses.

Question 33 ▷ One Gray is

A the absorbed dose of radiation per kilogram.

B measured in joules per kilogram.

C equivalent to 1000 rad.

D expected to produce a rise in temperature of 10°C per kilogram.

E also used to measure radiation in obstetric ultrasound.

Question 34 ▷ The following types of ionising radiation are have high linear energy transfer (LET):

A neutron beam.

B alpha particles.

C heavy ions.

D X-rays.

E γ-rays.

Question 35 ▷ The effects of radiotherapy on a tumour are

A increased by hypoxia.

B usually increased by an inadequate blood supply which results in hypoxia.

C increased by oxygenation.

D dependent upon the radiosensitivity of the tumour.

E due to damage to the DNA in the cells.

Question 36 ▷ Radiation-induced damage to the cell includes

A double-strand break of DNA.

B single-strand break of DNA.

C formation of intrastrand cross links within DNA.

D formation of DNA interstrand cross links.

E formation of cross links between DNA and nuclear proteins.

Question 37 ▷ DNA contains

A 2-deoxy-D-ribose.
B phosphate esters.
C uracil.
D uridine.
E deoxythymidine.

Question 38 ▷ The following are examples of conditions where both alleles must be mutated to cause the disease:

A Tay Sachs disease.
B congenital adrenal hyperplasia.
C vitamin D-resistant rickets.
D haemophilia A.
E Edwards syndrome.

Question 39 ▷ A woman who is a gene carrier for cystic fibrosis marries a man who is also a gene carrier for cystic fibrosis. The risks to their offspring can be stated as follows:

A The risk of an affected child is one in four.
B The risk of an affected son is one in four.
C The risk of an affected daughter is one in four.
D The risk of a child who is a carrier is greater than the gene frequency of the condition in a North European population.
E If they have an affected son, the risk to the child in the next pregnancy of having the condition is one in eight.

Question 40 ▷ The following are examples of single-gene disorders with an autosomal-dominant type of inheritance:

A myotonic dystrophy.
B Duchenne muscular dystrophy.
C anencephaly.
D Xg blood group.
E erythaema multiforme.

Question 41 ▷ The following conditions are inherited as an autosomal recessive:

A congenital adrenal hyperplasia due to 21 hydroxylase deficiency.
B glucose-6-phosphate dehydrogenase deficiency.
C nephrogenic diabetes insipidus.
D congenital talipes equino varus.
E β-thalassaemia.

Question 42 ▷ The following conditions are inherited as a X-linked dominant:

A achondroplasia.
B 47,XXX.
C 47,XXY.
D fragile X syndrome.
E holoprosencephaly.

Question 43 ▷ The following are examples of single-gene disorders with X-linked inheritance:

A galactosaemia.
B glucose-6-phosphate dehydrogenase deficiency.
C vitamin D-resistant rickets.
D Lesch–Nyhan syndrome.
E cutaneous lichen sclerosus (CREST syndrome).

Question 44 ▷ The following steps are necessary for the processing of pre-mRNA to mRNA:

A binding with small nuclear ribonucleoproteins.
B removal of introns.
C joining of exons.
D polyadenylation.
E topoisomerisation.

Question 45 ▷ Tetanus

A is caused by the release of an endotoxin.
B may result from infection of the umbilical stump of the newborn.
C leads to flaccid paralysis.
D is effectively prevented by using an attenuated vaccine prepared from the causative organism.
E is associated with overactivity of the sympathetic nervous system.

Question 46 ▷ Vaccines are available against:

A tuberculosis.
B syphilis.
C gonorrhoea.
D tetanus.
E diphtheria.

Question 47 ▷ The BCG vaccine

A induces cell-mediated immunity.
B is an example of an attenuated bacterial vaccine.
C contains mycobacteria that often revert to virulence.
D must never be given to an infant aged less than 6 months.
E is effective at preventing tubercular meningitis.

Question 48 ▷ Wound healing is promoted by

A hypoxia.
B bacterial infection.
C corticosteroids.
D platelet degranulation.
E myofibroblasts.

Question 49 ▷ In cases of postmortem following maternal mortality, blocks for histological examination must be taken from the following organs as a minimum:

A spleen.
B femur.

C kidney.
D brain.
E supraclavicular lymph nodes.

Question 50 ▷ Creatinine clearance

A may be calculated from measurement of serum creatinine and the concentration of urinary creatinine.
B is approximately 120 ml/minute in the healthy adult.
C may be elevated to 190 ml/minute in a pregnant woman with diabetes who is taking insulin.
D is an approximate measure of the glomerular filtration rate.
E may be markedly elevated in the initial phase of acute renal failure.

Question 51 ▷ Primary syphilis

A appears as a painless genital ulcer within 1 week of infection.
B produces well-defined and indurated lesions.
C produces lesions prior to seroconversion.
D produces lesions in the genital area only.
E is followed by a period of asymptomatic latency.

Question 52 ▷ The following conditions are premalignant:

A balanitis xerotica obliterans.
B syphilitic chancre.
C xeroderma pigmentosum.
D Paget's disease of bone.
E ulcerative colitis.

Question 53 ▷ Examples of carcinogens include:

A ionising radiation.
B 3,4-benzpyrene.
C β-naphthylamine.
D oxytocin.
E ergotamine.

Question 54 ▷ Characteristics of a malignant neoplasm include:
A resemblance to tissue of origin.
B well-circumscribed border.
C necrotic areas.
D invasion of surrounding tissues.
E normal nuclear morphology.

Question 55 ▷ The following are examples of tumours of epithelial origin:
A melanoma.
B adenocarcinoma.
C squamous carcinoma.
D hepatoblastoma.
E rhabdomyosarcoma.

Question 56 ▷ The following are examples of tumours of mesenchymal origin:
A osteoma.
B chondroma.
C lipoma.
D neurofibroma.
E squamous papilloma.

Question 57 ▷ The following conditions are uniformly lethal:
A anencephaly.
B Down syndrome.
C Edwards syndrome.
D Patau syndrome.
E β-thalassaemia trait.

Question 58 ▷ Gonorrhoea is a cause of
A epididymitis.
B endocarditis.
C encephalitis.
D gummatous necrosis of the liver.
E cutaneous lesions.

Question 59 ▷ Visceral leishmaniasis
A is caused by *Leishmania donovani.*
B depends on the mosquito to act as a vector.
C is a cause of massive splenomegaly.
D may lead to liver failure if untreated.
E is treated by aminoglycosides.

Question 60 ▷ Normal bile contains
A cholesterol.
B bilirubin.
C biliverdin.
D stercobilin.
E urobilin.

Question 61 ▷ In the normal adult's electrocardiogram, the
A P wave represents the pressure in the right atrium.
B QRS complex represents ventricular depolarisation.
C PR interval varies between 1 and 2 seconds.
D ST segment represents atrial repolarisation.
E T wave represents ventricular repolarisation.

Question 62 ▷ A healthy pregnant woman travels by helicopter from sea level to an altitude of 4000 metres. The physiological changes which would be evident within 30 minutes include
A increased alveolar ventilation rate.
B increased pulmonary blood flow.
C hypercapnia.
D fall in arterial pH.
E increased vascularity of peripheral tissues.

Question 63 ▷ Growth hormone secretion is increased by
A kwashiorkor.
B testosterone.
C estradiol.
D somatostatin.
E increased level of free fatty acids in the blood.

Question 64 ▷ Aldosterone

A is an example of a steroid hormone.
B contains 21 carbon atoms in each molecule.
C is derived from Δ^5 pregnenolone.
D is synthesised in the cells of the zona fasciculata of the adrenal cortex.
E synthesis is inhibited by acetylcholine.

Question 65 ▷ During normal pregnancy in a healthy woman, the anterior pituitary gland

A decreases in size.
B secretes significantly less follicle stimulating hormone (FSH).
C secretes significantly less luteinising hormone (LH).
D increases secretion of prolactin.
E secretes less adrenocorticotrophic hormone (ACTH).

Question 66 ▷ The concentration of the following substances is higher in fetal blood than in maternal blood in a normal pregnancy in a healthy woman:

A riboflavin.
B vitamin B12.
C oxygen.
D calcium.
E basic amino acids.

Question 67 ▷ Renin

A is an enzyme.
B catalyses the reaction to convert angiotensinogen to angiotensin 1.
C is synthesised by hepatocytes.
D release is inhibited by nonsteroidal anti-inflammatory drugs.
E release is stimulated by adenosine.

Question 68 ▷ In a healthy supine woman, the mean pulmonary arterial pressure is higher than the mean pressure in the

A superior vena cava.
B pulmonary veins.
C uterine artery.
D left atrium.
E aortic arch.

6 | Standalone EMQ paper I (paper I type)

OPTIONS

A Abdominal aorta
B Common iliac artery
C External iliac artery
D Femoral artery
E Inferior mesenteric artery
F Internal iliac artery

Instructions

Select the **single** vessel which gives rise to the arteries in the human female listed in the items below. Each option may be used once, more than once or not at all.

Question I ▷ Ovarian artery.

Question 2 ▷ Middle rectal artery.

OPTIONS

	Arterial blood supply	Venous drainage	Secretion of progesterone
A	Left ovarian artery, branch of the abdominal aorta	Left ovarian vein leading to the left internal iliac vein	Mainly by the granulosa cells
B	Left ovarian artery, branch of the abdominal aorta	Left ovarian vein leading to the left renal vein	By the corpus luteum during the luteal phase
C	Left ovarian artery, branch of the left internal iliac artery	Left ovarian vein leading to the left internal iliac vein	By the corpus luteum during the follicular phase

	Arterial blood supply	Venous drainage	Secretion of progesterone
D	Left ovarian artery, branch of the left middle rectal artery	Left ovarian vein leading to the left renal vein	By the corpus luteum after fertilisation
E	Right ovarian artery, branch of the abdominal aorta	Right ovarian vein leading to the inferior vena cava	By the corpus luteum during the luteal phase
F	Right ovarian artery, branch of the abdominal aorta	Right ovarian vein leading to the inferior vena cava	Mainly by the granulosa cells
G	Right ovarian artery, branch of the right internal iliac artery	Right ovarian vein leading to the inferior vena cava	By the corpus luteum during the follicular phase
H	Right ovarian artery, branch of the right middle rectal artery	Right ovarian vein leading to the right internal iliac vein	By the corpus luteum after fertilisation

Instructions

The list of options shows different profiles of an organ. Choose the **single** correct description in terms of blood supply and secretion of progesterone for the item below.

Question 3 ▷ Right ovary.

OPTIONS

	Embryological origin	Connections
A	Metanephric blastema	Renal sinus to the base of the urinary bladder
B	Metanephric blastema	Renal sinus to the fundus of the urinary bladder
C	Ureteric bud from the mesonephric duct	Renal sinus to the base of the urinary bladder

	Embryological origin	Connections
D	Ureteric bud from the mesonephric duct	Renal sinus to the fundus of the urinary bladder
E	Ureteric bud from the paramesonephric duct	Renal sinus to the base of the bladder after fusion with a diverticulum
F	Ureteric bud from the paramesonephric duct	Renal sinus to the base of the urinary bladder
G	Ureteric bud from the paramesonephric duct	Renal sinus to the fundus of the urinary bladder
H	Ureteric diverticulum from the paramesonephric duct	Renal sinus to the base of the urinary bladder

Instructions

Select the **single** option which gives the best description of the structures in the item below.

Question 4 ▷ Left ureter in the adult female.

OPTIONS

A	80%	G	13%
B	70%	H	8%
C	60%	I	3.5%
D	40%	J	1%
E	25%	K	0.5%
F	20%	L	0.1%

Instructions

Select the **single** most correct proportion of fetal cardiac output which is distributed to the structures in the items below. Each option may be used once, more than once or not at all.

Question 5 ▷ Brain.

Question 6 ▷ Fetal adrenals.

OPTIONS

	Type of nucleic acid in genome	Teratogen	Vaccine
A	DNA	No	Available
B	DNA	Yes	Available
C	DNA	No	Unavailable
D	DNA	Yes	Unavailable
E	RNA	No	Available
F	RNA	Yes	Available
G	RNA	No	Unavailable
H	RNA	Yes	Unavailable

Instructions

The list of options describes viruses in terms of the type of nucleic acid contained in the genome, whether or not the virus is a teratogen in human pregnancy and whether or not a vaccine is available. Select the **single** correct profile for each of the viruses in the items below. Each option may be used once, more than once or not at all.

Question 7 ▷ Rubella.

Question 8 ▷ Human papillomavirus type 11.

OPTIONS

A *Borrelia burgdoferi*
B *Borrelia recurrentis*
C *Chlamydia pneumoniae*
D *Chlamydia psittaci*
E *Chlamydia trachomatis*

F *Haemophilus ducreyi*
G *Haemophilus haemolyticus*
H *Haemophilus parahaemolyticus*
I *Haemophilus paraphrophilus*
J *Mycobacterium leprae*
K *Mycobacterium tuberculosis*
L *Plasmodium falciparum*
M *Plasmodium vivax*
N *Treponema carateum*
O *Treponema pallidum* subspecies endemicum
P *Treponema pallidum* subspecies pallidum
Q *Treponema pallidum* subspecies pertenue
R *Trypanosoma brucei gambiense*
S *Trypanosoma cruzi*
T *Yersinia pestis*

Instructions

Select the **single** aetiological agent from the list of options for each of the human diseases listed in the item below.

Question 9 ▷ Bejel.

OPTIONS

A Day 2
B Day 10
C Day 14
D Day 22
E Day 25
F Day 28
G Day 33
H Day 40
I Day 44
J Day 50
K Day 60
L Day 61
M Day 62
N Day 64
O Day 68
P Day 70
Q Day 100
R Day 122
S Day 125
T Day 180

Instructions

The list of options refers to days after fertilisation in a human pregnancy. Select the **single** most appropriate time in embryological development for each stage in the formation of the eye referred to in the items below. Each option may be used once, more than once or not at all.

Question 10 ▷ Formation of the optic vesicles by evagination of the walls of the forebrain at the optic sulcus.

Question 11 ▷ Formation of the lens vesicle.

OPTIONS

A	0.1	I	30
B	1	J	50
C	2	K	100
D	3	L	150
E	4	M	200
F	5	N	500
G	10	O	1000
H	20	P	2000

Instructions

The activity of cortisol is '1'. Select the **single** relative corticosteroid activity of the items listed below from the list of options. Each option may be used once, more than once or not at all.

Question 12 ▷ Cortisone.

Question 13 ▷ Methylprednisolone.

OPTIONS

	Site of biosynthesis	Target organs	Effect on serum glucose
A	Alpha cells in the islets of Langerhans	Kidney	Elevated
B	Alpha cells in the islets of Langerhans	Liver	Elevated
C	Alpha cells in the islets of Langerhans	Liver	Lowered
D	Alpha cells in the islets of Langerhans	Liver, skeletal muscle	Elevated
E	Beta cells in the islets of Langerhans	Cardiac muscle	Lowered
F	Beta cells in the islets of Langerhans	Liver	Elevated
G	Beta cells in the islets of Langerhans	Liver, skeletal muscle	Lowered
H	Beta cells in the islets of Langerhans	Liver, skeletal muscle, adipose tissue	Lowered
I	Liver	Adrenal cortex	Lowered
J	Liver	Cardiac muscle	Elevated
K	Liver	Skeletal muscle, adipose tissue	Lowered
L	Liver	Smooth muscle	Elevated

Instructions

The list of options shows different metabolic profiles in terms of site of biosynthesis, target organ(s) and effect on serum glucose. Select the **single** profile that best describes the metabolic profiles of the hormone in the item below.

Question 14 ▷ Insulin.

OPTIONS

A Altered distribution
B Decreased absorption
C Increased urinary excretion
D Induction of a new mutation in cytochrome P450 genes
E Induction of cytochrome P450
F Inhibition of cytochrome P450
G Production of antibodies against specific drug receptor
H Underlying genetic polymorphism of cytochrome P450 genes

Instructions

The list of options refers to different factors which may affect drug metabolism. The items below refer to examples of drug metabolism. Select the **single** most likely mechanism for the item below.

Question 15 ▷ A woman with an excessive alcohol intake underwent an operation under general anaesthesia and received a standard dose of halothane. The operation itself was uncomplicated but the woman developed non-viral hepatitis.

OPTIONS

A Amoebicidal in plasma
B Blockage of protein kinase receptors
C Enhancement of radiosensitivity
D Enhancement of photosensitivity
E Increased biliary excretion
F Inhibition of retroviral fusion
G Inhibition of bacterial cell wall synthesis
H Inhibition of bacterial nucleic acid synthesis
I Inhibition of bacterial protein synthesis
J Inhibition of retroviral non-nucleoside reverse transcriptase

K Inhibition of retroviral nucleoside reverse transcriptase
L Inhibition of retroviral protease
M Initiation of an anaphylactic reaction
N Lysis of bacterial cell wall
O Production of beta lactamase
P Schizonticidal within erythrocytes
Q Schizonticidal within hepatocytes

Instructions

The list of options contains different pharmacological reactions. Select the **single** reaction which best describes the principal antimicrobial activity of the drugs in the items below. Each option may be used once, more than once or not at all.

Question 16 ▷ Benzyl penicillin.

Question 17 ▷ Abacavir.

OPTIONS

A 90
B 10
C 5
D 2

Instructions

A research team carried out a prospective study to examine the relationship between a viral pathogen (*V*) of the female genital tract and invasive cancer of the cervix. A causal relationship was suspected but not established. Two thousand women were studied following the appropriate permission from the regional ethics committee and the women's informed consent. None of the women had either premalignant or malignant disease of the cervix or evidence of infection by the viral pathogen at the start of the study. The study was carried out over a 10-year period and the results are summarised in the following table:

	Early stage invasive cancer of the cervix present	No evidence of invasive cancer of the cervix
Viral pathogen *V* infects genital tract	100	900
No evidence of infection by viral pathogen *V*	10	990

The list of options contains different values of relative risk.

Question 18 ▷ Calculate the relative risk of developing invasive cancer of the cervix following exposure to the viral pathogen *V* and select the value from the list of options.

OPTIONS

	Site of biosynthesis in the kidney	Action
A	Cells of the proximal renal tubule	Inhibition of calcium absorption from the gut
B	Cells of the proximal renal tubule	Initiation of multiple signalling pathways in erythrocyte precursors
C	Cells of the proximal renal tubule	Protease which uses angiotensin 1 as its substrate
D	Cells of the proximal renal tubule	Stimulation of calcium absorption from the gut
E	Juxtaglomerular apparatus	Protease which uses angiotensin 1 as its substrate
F	Juxtaglomerular apparatus	Protease which uses angiotensinogen as its substrate
G	Juxtaglomerular apparatus	Protease which uses haemoglobin as its substrate
H	Juxtaglomerular apparatus	Stimulation of calcium absorption from the gut

	Site of biosynthesis in the kidney	Action
I	Renal peritubular endothelial cells	Initiation of multiple signalling pathways in erythrocyte precursors
J	Renal peritubular endothelial cells	Initiation of multiple signalling pathways in erythrocytes
K	Renal peritubular endothelial cells	Initiation of multiple signalling pathways in hepatocytes
L	Renal peritubular endothelial cells	Stimulation of iron absorption from the gut

Instructions

The list of options gives descriptions of the renal sites of biosynthesis and actions of different molecules. Select the **single** most correct profile for the substance in the item below.

Question 19 ▷ Erythropoietin.

OPTIONS

A 0.01
B 0.025
C 0.03
D 0.04
E 0.05
F 0.06
G 0.07
H 0.075
I 0.078
J 0.1
K 0.25
L 0.3
M 0.4
N 0.5
O 0.6
P 0.7
Q 0.75
R 0.78
S 1.6
T 1.66

Instructions

Studies of various different sizes were carried out in healthy postmenopausal women. As part of the overall project, the systolic and diastolic blood pressures were measured reliably in all the women. The measurements showed a perfect Gaussian distribution. The list of options contains different values for standard error. The item below provides values of the number of women involved and a description of the central tendency of diastolic blood pressure. The study showed a perfect Gaussian distribution of the measurements of diastolic blood pressure. Select the **single** standard error for the study referred to in the item below. Each option may be used once, more than once or not at all.

Question 20 ▷ $N = 10{,}000$, mean = 70 mmHg, variance = 25.

7 | Standalone EMQ paper 2 (paper 2 type)

OPTIONS

A 10
B 18
C 28
D 100
E 150
F 280
G 300
H 350
I 450
J 540
K 550
L 700

Instructions

The list of options contains different values of the wavelength of light in nanometres. Select the absorbance maxima for the molecule in the item below.

Question 1 ▷ Tryptophan.

OPTIONS

A Metabolic acidosis
B Metabolic alkalosis
C Respiratory acidosis
D Respiratory alkalosis

Instructions

Select the **single** acid-base disorder which is most likely to be caused by the conditions in the items below. Each option may be used once, more than once or not at all.

Question 2 ▷ Hyperventilation due to anxiety in an otherwise pregnant healthy woman.

Question 3 ▷ Severe diarrhoea.

OPTIONS

A Early embryonic development
B Menopause
C Mid-trimester of pregnancy
D Onset of labour
E Ovulation
F Puberty

Instructions

The list of options refers to different stages during the life of a normal woman with a karyotype 46,XX. Select the **single** correct time of the events referred to in the items below. Each option may be used once, more than once or not at all.

Question 4 ▷ Inactivation of one of the X chromosomes.

Question 5 ▷ Follicular development and an increase in stroma.

OPTIONS

A Cardiomyopathy
B Dermatitis
C Encephalopathy
D Hepatic damage
E Nephropathy
F Neuropathy

Instructions

The list of options contains different toxicities. Select the **single** most likely toxicity which would result from excess exposure to the trace elements referred to in the items below. Each option may be used once, more than once or not at all.

Question 6 ▷ Mercury.

Question 7 ▷ Cobalt.

OPTIONS

A Adrenocortical cancer and melanoma
B Brain tumours, sarcoma of bone and soft tissue
C Breast cancer and ovarian cancer
D Breast cancer and retinoblastoma
E Breast cancer, brain tumours, adrenocortical cancer, leukaemia, sarcoma of bone and soft tissue
F Breast cancer, brain tumours, endometrial cancer
G Breast cancer, ovarian cancer, adrenocortical cancer, acute myeloid leukaemia
H Cancer of the rectum and cancer of the stomach
I Cancer of the rectum, cancer of the endometrium, cancer of the stomach and cancer of the bile duct
J Colonic cancer and cancer of the stomach
K Colorectal cancer and bronchopulmonary cancer
L Colorectal cancer, cancer of the endometrium, cancer of the stomach and cancer of the bile duct
M Ovarian cancer
N Ovarian cancer and retinoblastoma
O Retinoblastoma
P Retinoblastoma and adenocarcinoma of the cervix
Q Retinoblastoma and adrenocortical cancer
R Retinoblastoma and cancer of the bladder
S Retinoblastoma and cancer of the endometrium
T Retinoblastoma and osteosarcoma

Instructions

The list of options describes different malignant conditions. The items below refer to conditions which increase tumour susceptibility. Select the **single** option which indicates which tumour(s) an individual would be at increased risk of acquiring for each of the conditions in the items below. Each option may be used once, more than once or not at all.

Question 8 ▷ BRCA1.

Question 9 ▷ Li Fraumeni syndrome.

OPTIONS

A X chromosome
B Y chromosome
C Chromosome 1
D Chromosome 5
E Chromosome 7
F Chromosome 9
G Chromosome 11
H Chromosome 21
I Chromosome 2
J Chromosome 8
K Chromosome 12
L Chromosome 16
M Chromosome 20
N Chromosome 22

Instructions

Select the location of the gene referred to in the item below.

Question 10 ▷ Gene for the delta chain of haemoglobin.

OPTIONS

A Immunoglobulin A (IgA)
B Immunoglobulin D (IgD)
C Immunoglobulin E (IgE)
D Immunoglobulin G (IgG)
E Immunoglobulin M (IgM)

Instructions

Select the **single** immunoglobulin which has the function(s) in the item below.

Question 11 ▷ Opsonisation for neutrophils.

OPTIONS

A Chaga's disease
B Congenital adrenal hyperplasia
C Cystic fibrosis
D Galactosaemia
E Intestinal atresia
F Tay-Sachs disease

Instructions

Select the **single** disease which would result from the gene mutation described below from the list of options.

Question 12 ▷ A gene mutation results in the deletion of a phenylalanine residue in one of two nucleotide-binding domains in a transmembrane conductance regulatory protein. One of the metabolic consequences of the mutation is that there is excessive loss of chloride (Cl–) in sweat.

OPTIONS

A Acetic acid
B Alcian blue
C Alcian green
D Alcian red
E Aqueous iodine
F Background illumination
G Congo blue
H Congo red
I Gentian violet
J Gram stain
K Haematoxylin and eosin
L Lugol's iodine
M Martius scarlet blue
N Masson-Fontana
O Periodic Acid Schiff
P Ziehl Neelsen

Instructions

Select the **single** appropriate stain for each of the items referred to below from the list of options. Each option may be used once, more than once or not at all.

Question 13 ▷ Neutral mucin.

Question 14 ▷ Melanin pigment.

OPTIONS

	Type of inheritance	Enzyme defect
A	Autosomal dominant	Glucocerebrosidase
B	Autosomal dominant	Hexosaminidase A
C	Autosomal dominant	Phenylalanine hydroxylase
D	Autosomal dominant	Sphingomyelinase
E	Autosomal recessive	Glucocerebrosidase
F	Autosomal recessive	Hexosaminidase A
G	Autosomal recessive	Phenylalanine hydroxylase
H	Autosomal recessive	Sphingomyelinase
I	X-linked dominant	Glucocerebrosidase
J	X-linked dominant	Hexosaminidase A
K	X-linked dominant	Phenylalanine hydroxylase
L	X-linked dominant	Sphingomyelinase
M	X-linked recessive	Glucocerebrosidase
N	X-linked recessive	Hexosaminidase A
O	X-linked recessive	Phenylalanine hydroxylase
P	X-linked recessive	Sphingomyelinase

Instructions

Select the **single** option that describes the type of inheritance and the enzyme defect for each of the metabolic defects in the items below. Each option may be used once, more than once or not at all.

Question 15 ▷ Tay-Sachs disease.

Question 16 ▷ Niemann Pick disease.

OPTIONS

	Secretion of insulin	Secretion of glucagon
A	Increased	Increased
B	Increased	Decreased
C	Decreased	Increased
D	Decreased	Decreased

Instructions

The list of options describes different responses in the secretion of insulin and in the secretion of glucagon by a healthy adult. Select the **single** appropriate responses for each of the items below. Each option may be used once, more than once or not at all.

Question 17 ▷ Elevation in blood sugar.

Question 18 ▷ Somatostatin.

OPTIONS

A 7
B 14
C 20
D 50
E 70
F 100
G 110
H 140
I 180
J 200
K 220
L 230

Instructions

The list of options provides different values for creatinine clearance in ml/minute. Calculate the creatinine clearance using the data provided in the items below and select the **single** closest value for each item from the list of options. Each option may be used once, more than once or not at all.

Question 19 ▷ Serum creatinine = 60 μmol/l, urine creatinine = 6 mmol/l, urine volume in 24 hours = 2 litres.

Question 20 ▷ Serum creatinine = 100 μmol/l, urine creatinine = 1 mmol/l, urine volume in 24 hours = 1 litre.

8 | Standalone EMQ paper 3 (paper I type)

OPTIONS

	Inflow	Outflow
A	Two pulmonary veins	Left ventricle
B	Four pulmonary veins	Ductus venosus
C	Four pulmonary veins	Left ventricle
D	Coronary sulcus	Left ventricle
E	Inferior vena cava	Right ventricle
F	Superior vena cava	Right ventricle
G	Superior vena cava and inferior vena cava	Ductus arteriosus
H	Superior vena cava and inferior vena cava	Right ventricle

Instructions

Select the option that provides the best description of blood flow in the cardiac chambers of the adult heart referred to in the items below. Each option may be used once, more than once or not at all.

Question 1 ▷ Right atrium.

Question 2 ▷ Left atrium.

OPTIONS

	Embryological origin	Connections
A	Metanephric blastema	Renal sinus to the base of the urinary bladder
B	Metanephric blastema	Renal sinus to the fundus of the urinary bladder
C	Ureteric bud from the mesonephric duct	Renal sinus to the base of the urinary bladder
D	Ureteric bud from the mesonephric duct	Renal sinus to the fundus of the urinary bladder
E	Ureteric bud from the paramesonephric duct	Renal sinus to the base of the bladder after fusion with a diverticulum
F	Ureteric bud from the paramesonephric duct	Renal sinus to the base of the urinary bladder
G	Ureteric bud from the paramesonephric duct	Renal sinus to the fundus of the urinary bladder
H	Ureteric diverticulum from the paramesonephric duct	Renal sinus to the base of the urinary bladder

Instructions

Select the **single** option which gives the best description of the structures in the item below.

Question 3 ▷ Right ureter in the adult female.

OPTIONS

	Arterial blood supply	Venous drainage	Secretion of progesterone
A	Left ovarian artery, branch of the abdominal aorta	Left ovarian vein leading to the left internal iliac vein	Mainly by the granulosa cells
B	Left ovarian artery, branch of the abdominal aorta	Left ovarian vein leading to the left renal vein	By the corpus luteum during the luteal phase
C	Left ovarian artery, branch of the left internal iliac artery	Left ovarian vein leading to the left internal iliac vein	By the corpus luteum during the follicular phase
D	Left ovarian artery, branch of the left middle rectal artery	Left ovarian vein leading to the left renal vein	By the corpus luteum after fertilisation
E	Right ovarian artery, branch of the abdominal aorta	Right ovarian vein leading to the inferior vena cava	By the corpus luteum during the luteal phase
F	Right ovarian artery, branch of the abdominal aorta	Right ovarian vein leading to the inferior vena cava	Mainly by the granulosa cells
G	Right ovarian artery, branch of the right internal iliac artery	Right ovarian vein leading to the inferior vena cava	By the corpus luteum during the follicular phase
H	Right ovarian artery, branch of the right middle rectal artery	Right ovarian vein leading to the right internal iliac vein	By the corpus luteum after fertilisation

Instructions

The list of options shows different profiles of an organ. Choose the **single** correct description in terms of blood supply and secretion of progesterone for the item below.

Question 4 ▷ Left ovary.

OPTIONS

A Coelomic wall epithelium
B Endoderm epithelium
C Mesenchyme
D Neural crest
E Neural plate epithelium
F Surface ectoderm epithelium

Instructions

The list of options refers to specific epithelial and mesenchymal cell populations in the early human embryo. Select the **single** origin of the structures referred to in the items from the list of options. Each option may be used once, more than once or not at all.

Question 5 ▷ Hepatocytes.

Question 6 ▷ Connective tissue of the ovary.

OPTIONS

A	0.01	I	300
B	0.1	J	500
C	2	K	900
D	5	L	1000
E	10	M	1200
F	100	N	2000
G	150	O	9000
H	200	P	10,000

Instructions

The androgenic activity of testosterone is '100'. For each of the androgens in the items below select the level of androgenic activity from the list of options. Each option may be used once, more than once or not at all.

Question 7 ▷ Dihydrotestosterone.

Question 8 ▷ Dehydroepiandrosterone.

OPTIONS

A Adrenal cortex
B Adrenal medulla
C Anterior lobe of the pituitary gland
D Arcuate nuclei of the hypothalamus
E Caudate nuclei
F Cerebellum
G Cerebral cortex
H Hippocampus
I Islets of Langerhans in the pancreas
J Liver
K Median eminence
L Optic chiasm
M Ovary
N Pituitary stalk
O Posterior lobe of the pituitary gland
P Renal peritubular endothelial cells
Q Spleen
R Supraoptic and paraventricular nuclei of the hypothalamus
S Thymus
T Ventromedial nuclei of the hypothalamus

Instructions

The items below refer to various molecules which affect human metabolism. Select the site of production of each item from the list of options. Each option may be used once, more than once or not at all.

Question 9 ▷ Glucagon.

Question 10 ▷ Follicle-stimulating hormone.

OPTIONS

A *Borrelia burgdoferi*
B *Borrelia recurrentis*
C *Chlamydia pneumoniae*

D *Chlamydia psittaci*
E *Chlamydia trachomatis*
F *Haemophilus ducreyi*
G *Haemophilus haemolyticus*
H *Haemophilus parahaemolyticus*
I *Haemophilus paraphrophilus*
J *Mycobacterium leprae*
K *Mycobacterium tuberculosis*
L *Plasmodium falciparum*
M *Plasmodium vivax*
N *Treponema carateum*
O *Treponema pallidum* subspecies endemicum
P *Treponema pallidum* subspecies pallidum
Q *Treponema pallidum* subspecies pertenue
R *Trypanosoma brucei gambiense*
S *Trypanosoma cruzi*
T *Yersinia pestis*

Instructions

Select the **single** aetiological agent from the list of options for each of the human diseases listed in the item below.

Question 11 ▷ Pinta.

OPTIONS

A Amoebicidal in plasma
B Blockage of protein kinase receptors
C Enhancement of radiosensitivity
D Enhancement of photosensitivity
E Increased biliary excretion
F Inhibition of retroviral fusion
G Inhibition of bacterial cell wall synthesis
H Inhibition of bacterial nucleic acid synthesis
I Inhibition of bacterial protein synthesis

J Inhibition of retroviral non-nucleoside reverse transcriptase
K Inhibition of retroviral nucleoside reverse transcriptase
L Inhibition of retroviral protease
M Initiation of an anaphylactic reaction
N Lysis of bacterial cell wall
O Production of beta lactamase
P Schizonticidal within erythrocytes
Q Schizonticidal within hepatocytes

Instructions

The list of options contains different pharmacological reactions. Select the **single** reaction which best describes the principal antimicrobial activity of the drugs in the items below. Each option may be used once, more than once or not at all.

Question 12 ▷ Methicillin.

Question 13 ▷ Primaquine.

OPTIONS

A Androgen
B Antibiotic
C Antifibrinolytic
D Antimycotic
E Antiestrogen
F Antiprogesterone
G Fibrinolytic
H Estrogen
I Oxytocic alkaloid
J Progestogen
K Prostaglandin analogue
L Prostaglandin synthetase inhibitor
M Steroid estrogen receptor modulating agent
N Tocolytic

Instructions

Select the type of drug from the list of options for each of the drugs in the items below. Each option may be used once, more than once or not at all.

Question 14 ▷ Tamoxifen.

Question 15 ▷ Atosiban.

Question 16 ▷ Norethisterone.

OPTIONS

A 0.2

B 0.67

C 1

D 10

E 20

F 45

G 90

H 100

Instructions

A screening test for intrauterine growth restriction (IUGR) was devised, based on a composite score of maternal and fetal biometric data. A study was carried to compare the screening test with the actual birth weight against gestation in *N* women. The results of the study are presented in the table below:

Screen	IUGR present	IUGR absent
Positive	*w*	*y*
Negative	*x*	*z*

Each of the items below provide different values for *N*, *w*, *x*, *y* and *z*. Calculate the approximate likelihood ratio for each study and select the **single** correct answer from the list of options. Each option may be used once, more than once or not at all.

Question 17 ▷ $N = 200$, $w = 50$, $x = 50$, $y = 50$, $z = 50$.

Question 18 ▷ $N = 300$, $w = 90$, $x = 10$, $y = 2$, $z = 98$.

OPTIONS

A	2 mmHg	H	9 mmHg
B	3 mmHg	I	10 mmHg
C	4 mmHg	J	16 mmHg
D	5 mmHg	K	25 mmHg
E	6 mmHg	L	30 mmHg
F	7 mmHg	M	31 mmHg
G	8 mmHg	N	32 mmHg

Instructions

For each of the studies below, calculate and select the **single** correct standard deviation from the list of options. Each of the studies refer to systolic blood pressure in normal healthy pregnant women, the measurements of systolic blood pressure show a perfect Gaussian distribution and N = the number of women in each study. Each option may be used once, more than once or not at all.

Question 19 ▷ N= 500, mean = 100 mmHg, variance = 9.

Question 20 ▷ N= 50, mean = 105 mm Hg, variance = 64.

9 | Standalone EMQ paper 4 (paper 2 type)

OPTIONS

	Biosynthetic pathway	Serum binding	Absorption of light (nm)
A	Produced as a result of the action of biliverdin reductase on haeme	Albumin	450
B	Produced by glucuronidation	Cortisol-binding globulin	550
C	Produced by the action of 7-α-hydroxylase (CYP7A1) on taurocholic acid	Albumin	280
D	Produced by the action of 7-α-hydroxylase (CYP7A1) on glycocholic acid	Transferrin	550
E	Produced as a result of the action of biliverdin reductase on biliverdin	Albumin	450

Instructions

The list of options provides metabolic profiles which describe pathway of biosynthesis, what the substance binds to in human serum and the wavelength at which maximum absorption of light occurs. Select the **single** correct profile for the item below.

Question 1 ▷ Bilirubin.

OPTIONS

A Activation of plasminogen to plasmin
B Antiplatelet activity
C Degradation of fibrin to fibrin degradation products
D Endotoxic shock
E Inactivation of free plasmin
F Inactivation of thrombin
G Stimulation of platelet adhesiveness
H Vasoconstriction

Instructions

Select the mechanism of action of the substances in the items below. Each option may be used once, more than once or not at all.

Question 2 ▷ Streptokinase.

Question 3 ▷ α-2 antiplasmin

OPTIONS

A Antiport
B ATP-mediated diffusion
C Carrier-mediated diffusion
D Channel-mediated diffusion
E Simple diffusion
F Solvent drag
G Symport
H Voltage-gated ion channel

Instructions

A research team has discovered different types of new molecules and is studying their transport across plasma membranes. Some experimental data are provided in the items below. The list of options contains different types of membrane transport. Select the **single** most appropriate option for each item. Each option may be used once, more than once or not at all.

Question 4 ▷ The molecules appear to move across the membrane from high to low concentration at a maximum rate of 10^7 per second. Inhibition of Na^+, K^+ – ATPase has no effect on transport.

Question 5 ▷ The molecules appear to move against an electrochemical gradient whereas molecules with a very similar structure do not cross the membrane at all. Inhibition of Na^+, K^+ – ATPase stops transport completely.

OPTIONS

A	1000	K	20,000
B	2000	L	22,000
C	9000	M	50,000
D	10,000	N	64,000
E	11,500	O	64,500
F	14,000	P	100,000
G	14,500	Q	200,000
H	15,000	R	300,000
I	15,100	S	500,000
J	16,000	T	640,500

Instructions

The items below refer to different molecules. Select the closest **single** approximate molecular weight for each molecule from the list of options. Each option may be used once, more than once or not at all.

Question 6 ▷ β chain of haemoglobin.

Question 7 ▷ Growth hormone.

OPTIONS

	Type of inheritance	Enzyme defect
A	Autosomal dominant	Glucose 6 phosphatase
B	Autosomal dominant	Iduronate sulphatase
C	Autosomal dominant	Lysosomal acid α1,4-glucosidase
D	Autosomal dominant	α-L-iduronidase
E	Autosomal recessive	Glucose 6 phosphatase
F	Autosomal recessive	Iduronate sulphatase
G	Autosomal recessive	Lysosomal acid α1,4-glucosidase
H	Autosomal recessive	α-L-iduronidase
I	X-linked dominant	Glucose 6 phosphatase
J	X-linked dominant	Iduronate sulphatase
K	X-linked dominant	Lysosomal acid α1,4-glucosidase
L	X-linked dominant	α-L-iduronidase
M	X-linked recessive	Glucose 6 phosphatase
N	X-linked recessive	Iduronate sulphatase
O	X-linked recessive	Lysosomal acid α1,4-glucosidase
P	X-linked recessive	α-L-iduronidase

Instructions

Select the option that describes the type of inheritance and enzyme defect in each of the metabolic disorders referred to in the items below. Each option may be used once, more than once or not at all.

Question 8 ▷ Von Gierke's disease.

Question 9 ▷ Hunter syndrome.

OPTIONS

	Probe	Target
A	Antibody	DNA
B	Antibody	Protein
C	Antibody	RNA
D	Nucleotide	DNA
E	Nucleotide	Protein
F	Nucleotide	RNA
G	Virus	DNA
H	Virus	RNA

Instructions

Select the option which shows the correct probe for a certain target for the laboratory method in the item below.

Question 10 ▷ Northern blot.

OPTIONS

A Immunoglobulin A (IgA)
B Immunoglobulin D (IgD)
C Immunoglobulin (IgE)
D Immunoglobulin (IgG)
E Immunoglobulin (IgM)

Instructions

Select the **single** immunoglobulin which has the function in the item below.

Question 11 ▷ Defence of mucosal surfaces.

OPTIONS

A Acrodermatitis enteropathica
B Cardiomyopathy
C Encephalopathy
D Goitre
E Hepatic damage
F Nephropathy
G Subacute combined degeneration of the spinal cord
H Suppression of the bone marrow

Instructions

Select the **single** most likely effect of the deficiency of the trace element referred to in the item below. Each option may be used once, more than once or not at all.

Question 12 ▷ Zinc.

OPTIONS

A Acetic acid
B Alcian blue
C Alcian green
D Alcian red
E Aqueous iodine
F Background illumination
G Congo blue
H Congo red
I Gentian violet
J Gram stain
K Haematoxylin and eosin
L Lugol's iodine
M Martius scarlet blue
N Masson-Fontana
O Periodic Acid Schiff
P Ziehl Neelsen

Instructions

Select the **single** appropriate stain for each of the items referred to below from the list of options. Each option may be used once, more than once or not at all.

Question 13 ▷ Amyloid.

Question 14 ▷ *Listeria monocytogenes.*

OPTIONS

A 40
B 44
C 70
D 80
E 90
F 100
G 110
H 120
I 130
J 140
K 150
L 160
M 170
N 180
O 190
P 200

Instructions

The list of options refers to temperature in degrees Celsius. The items below refer to degrees of tissue injury. Select the temperature at which the degree of tissue injury will occur from the list of options. Each option may be used once, more than once or not at all.

Question 15 ▷ Carbonisation.

Question 16 ▷ Coagulation.

OPTIONS

A Colon
B Duodenum and jejunum
C Ileum
D Oesophagus
E Rectum
F Stomach

Instructions

Select the **single** principal site at which the nutrients in the items are absorbed. Each option may be used once, more than once or not at all.

Question 17 ▷ Iron.

Question 18 ▷ Sodium chloride.

OPTIONS

A Albumin
B Caeruloplasmin
C Ferritin
D Fetal haemoglobin
E Haemoglobin A
F Haemoglobin S
G Human chorionic gonadotrophin
H Methaemoglobin
I Myoglobin
J Transferrin

Instructions

Select the protein which has the highest affinity for the elements in the items below. Each option may be used once, more than once or not at all.

Question 19 ▷ Oxygen.

Question 20 ▷ Copper.

10 | Answers to full paper 1 (Chapter 4)

EMQ SECTION

1 ▶ *B* = Frontal lobe.

2 ▶ *E* = Parietal lobe.

3 ▶ *H* = 25 cm.

4 ▶ *D* = 5 cm.

5 ▶ *C* = Day 3.

6 ▶ *I* = Day 13.

7 ▶ *I* = Zona fasciculata of the adrenal gland; Cortisol.

8 ▶ *C* = Corpus luetum of the ovary; Progesterone.

9 ▶ *J* = Thyroid gland (parafollicular C cells); Lowered.

10 ▶ *D* = Parathyroid gland (chief cells); Elevated.

11 ▶ *A* = DNA; Transplacental.

12 ▶ *P* = *Treponema pallidum* subspecies pallidum.

13 ▶ *A* = *Borrelia burgdoferi.*

14 ▶ *B* = Carbonic anhydrase inhibitor; Proximal tubule.

15 ▶ *N* = Osmotic; Loop of Henle.

16 ▶ *B* = Decreased absorption.

17 ▶ *C* = 1.

18 ▶ *I* = 400.

19 ▶ *B* = 3 mmHg.

20 ▶ *C* = 4 mmHg.

21 ▶ The vulva comprises the following:

A = Bartholin's gland. TRUE

B = labium majus. TRUE

C = labia minora. TRUE

D = anus. FALSE

E = clitoris. TRUE

22 ▶ The arterial blood supply to the vulva includes the

A = deep circumflex iliac artery. FALSE

B = median sacral artery. FALSE

C = superficial external pudendal artery. TRUE

D = deep external pudendal artery. TRUE

E = internal pudendal artery. TRUE

23 ▶ The diaphragm

A = receives its motor nerve supply from the lower six intercostal nerves. FALSE

B = has a concave upper surface. FALSE

C = has an aortic aperture at the level of the eighth thoracic vertebra. FALSE

D = is capable of lending additional power to all expulsive efforts. TRUE

E = is continuous with the outer layer of the muscle of the oesophagus. FALSE

24 ▶ The vagina receives arterial blood supply from the following branches of the internal iliac artery:

A = vaginal.	TRUE
B = superior vesical.	FALSE
C = uterine.	TRUE
D = obturator.	FALSE
E = internal pudendal.	TRUE

25 ▶ The following are branches of the abdominal aorta:

A = uterine artery.	FALSE
B = femoral artery.	FALSE
C = inferior phrenic artery.	TRUE
D = median sacral artery.	TRUE
E = coeliac trunk.	TRUE

26 ▶ The anal canal

A = is approximately 5 cm long in the adult.	FALSE
B = is lined by columnar epithelium along its whole length.	FALSE
C = is lined by keratinised stratified squamous epithelium along its lower half.	FALSE
D = is supplied by the median sacral arteries.	FALSE
E = contains the valves of Houston.	FALSE

27 ▶ The vagina

A = is innervated by the pelvic splanchnic nerves. TRUE

B = has on outer circular layer of muscle. FALSE

C = has an inner longitudinal layer of muscle. FALSE

D = is surrounded by skeletal muscle in its lower part. TRUE

E = has a posterior wall which is covered by peritoneum over its upper and internal quarter. TRUE

28 ▶ The uterus

A = weighs approximately 200 grams in a healthy nonpregnant adult woman. FALSE

B = weighs approximately 1 kg without contents at 40 weeks of gestation in a healthy pregnancy. TRUE

C = contains lymph vessels which diminish significantly in size during a normal pregnancy. FALSE

D = receives its main blood supply from the uterine artery. TRUE

E = is drained partly by the lateral aortic nodes. TRUE

29 ▶ The pelvic ureter

A = lies in extraperitoneal areolar tissue. TRUE

B = descend on the pelvic side wall along the anterior border of the greater sciatic notch. TRUE

C = lies inferior to the uterine artery and superior to the lateral vaginal fornix. TRUE

D = lies superior to both the uterine vein and the lateral vaginal fornix. FALSE

E = lies lateral to the inferior vesical artery and is 2 cm lateral to the internal cervical os at the level of the vaginal fornix. FALSE

30 ▶ The uterine artery

A = is a branch of the anterior division of the internal iliac artery.	TRUE
B = gives rise to an ascending branch which anastomoses with the tubal branch of the ovarian artery.	TRUE
C = gives rise to a descending branch which supplies the rectum.	FALSE
D = is separated from the uterine vein by the ureter.	FALSE
E = carries deoxygenated maternal blood during pregnancy.	FALSE

31 ▶ The paramesonephric ducts

A = lie lateral to the mesonephric ducts over most of their lengths at the time of their formation.	TRUE
B = begin to form at 6 weeks.	TRUE
C = begin to form before the mesonephric ducts.	FALSE
D = contain germ cells.	FALSE
E = give rise to the lower third of the ureter.	FALSE

32 ▶ The endoderm epithelium gives rise to the following:

A = hepatocytes.	TRUE
B = epithelial lining of the vesical trigone.	FALSE
C = β cells of the islets of Langerhans.	TRUE
D = peritoneum of greater omentum.	FALSE
E = peritoneum of lesser omentum.	FALSE

33 ▶ The embryonic mesenchyme gives rise to the following:

A = myometrium.	TRUE
B = pharyngeal glands.	FALSE
C = hepatocytes.	FALSE
D = cerebellum.	FALSE
E = basophils.	TRUE

34 ▶ The surface ectoderm epithelium gives rise to the following:

A = epithelium of the cornea.	TRUE
B = pubic hair.	TRUE
C = lining of the urinary bladder.	FALSE
D = epithelial lining of the vesical trigone.	FALSE
E = cerebellum.	FALSE

35 ▶ The neural crest gives rise to the following:

A = melanocytes.	TRUE
B = odontoblasts.	TRUE
C = hypodermis of face.	TRUE
D = dermis of face.	TRUE
E = pia mater.	TRUE

36 ▶ The adrenal cortex is the site of biosynthesis of

A = cortisol.	TRUE
B = adrenaline.	FALSE
C = vasopressin.	FALSE
D = dehydroepiandrosterone.	TRUE
E = aldosterone.	TRUE

37 ▶ Adrenocorticotrophic hormone (ACTH)

A = is secreted by the anterior lobe of the pituitary gland.	TRUE
B = is secreted in response to corticotrophin-releasing hormone.	TRUE
C = exerts its major action on the cells of the adrenal medulla.	FALSE
D = activates melanocyte-stimulating hormone receptors.	TRUE
E = is composed of two subunits.	FALSE

38 ▶ Growth hormone

A = stimulates the biosynthesis of insulin-like growth factors in the liver.	TRUE
B = inhibits the biosynthesis of insulin-like growth factors in the chondrocytes.	FALSE
C = inhibits the biosynthesis of insulin-like growth factors in muscle.	FALSE
D = stimulates lipolysis.	TRUE
E = inhibits gluconeogenesis in muscle.	FALSE

39 ▶ Follicle-stimulating hormone

A = is a glycoprotein.	TRUE
B = has a molecular weight of 30,000.	TRUE
C = is secreted by the anterior lobe of the pituitary gland.	TRUE
D = stimulates the seminiferous tubules in the male.	TRUE
E = is antagonised by insulin.	FALSE

40 ▶ Thyroid-stimulating hormone

A = is a lipoprotein. FALSE

B = contains 20,000 amino acids. FALSE

C = binds to a specific receptor on the basal membrane of epithelial cells of the thyroid gland. TRUE

D = stimulates the biosynthesis of thyroid hormones T3 and T4. TRUE

E = stimulates the release of thyroid hormones T3 and T4. TRUE

41 ▶ The following substances are released from the hypothalamus:

A = gonadotrophin-releasing hormone (GnRH). TRUE

B = Thyrotropin-releasing hormone (TRH). TRUE

C = Corticotrophin-like intermediary peptide (CLIP). FALSE

D = Angiotensinogen. FALSE

E = Follicle-stimulating hormone. FALSE

42 ▶ The pancreas secretes the following:

A = gastrin G-34. FALSE

B = trypsin. TRUE

C = carboxypolypeptidase. TRUE

D = intrinsic factor. FALSE

E = renin. FALSE

43 ▶ Insulin

A = is produced in the β-cells of the islets of Langerhans in the pancreas.	TRUE
B = is composed of two amino acid chains.	TRUE
C = has a plasma half-life that is approximately 6 minutes.	TRUE
D = is degraded mainly by the kidney.	FALSE
E = activity is enhanced by insulinase.	FALSE

44 ▶ Insulin secretion is increased by:

A = glucagon.	TRUE
B = cortisol.	TRUE
C = growth hormone.	TRUE
D = sulphonylureas.	TRUE
E = stimulation of α-adrenergic receptors by noradrenaline.	FALSE

45 ▶ Aldosterone

A = is synthesised in the cells of the adrenal medulla.	FALSE
B = binds to receptors on the cells of the distal tubule of the kidney.	TRUE
C = enhances the renal tubular reabsorption of sodium Na^+.	TRUE
D = increases the urinary excretion of potassium K^+.	TRUE
E = enhances the renal tubular reabsorption of hydrogen H^+.	FALSE

46 ▶ The following infections are paired correctly with the causal organism:

A = syphilis : *Haemophilus ducrei.*	FALSE
B = lymphogranuloma venereum : *mycobacterium tuberculosis.*	FALSE
C = gonorrhoea : *Trichomonas vaginalis.*	FALSE
D = malaria : *Plasmodium vivax.*	TRUE
E = scabies : *Herpes simplex virus.*	FALSE

47 ▶ *Candida albicans*

A = is a dimorphic fungus.	TRUE
B = forms hyphae when invasive.	TRUE
C = is the cause of histoplasmosis.	FALSE
D = is sensitive to broad spectrum antibiotics.	FALSE
E = is a cause of chorioamnionitis.	FALSE

48 ▶ Giardia lambia

A = may infect the pregnant woman.	TRUE
B = has specific molecules for attachment to the microvilli of epithelial cells.	TRUE
C = has a microvillar sucking disc.	TRUE
D = may cause severe diarrhoea.	TRUE
E = is sensitive to metronidazole.	TRUE

49 ▶ Gonorrhoea is a cause of

A = urethritis in women.	TRUE
B = urethritis in men.	TRUE
C = systemic lupus erythaematosus.	FALSE
D = chancres.	FALSE
E = condyloma accuminatum.	FALSE

50 ▶ Bacteria may acquire virulence by

A = transduction.	TRUE
B = reduced penicillin binding.	FALSE
C = plasmid transfer, which enables production of protease against immunoglobulin A (IgA).	FALSE
D = plasmid transfer, which enables production of lipopolysaccharide in the cell wall.	FALSE
E = insertion of a transposon which enables coating with fibronectin.	FALSE

51 ▶ Viruses

A = contain either DNA or RNA.	TRUE
B = do not possess a cell wall.	TRUE
C = can only replicate in living cells.	TRUE
D = do not possess mitochondria.	TRUE
E = possess ribosomes.	FALSE

52 ▶ The following organisms are part of the normal flora in the stomach:

A = lactobacilli.	TRUE
B = *Escherichia coli.*	FALSE
C = enterobacteria.	FALSE
D = vibrio cholera.	FALSE
E = *Taenia solium.*	FALSE

53 ▶ The following drugs are likely to lower the serum glucose:

A = β-adrenergic receptor antagonists.	TRUE
B = salicylates.	TRUE
C = bromocriptine.	TRUE
D = adrenaline.	FALSE
E = insulin.	TRUE

54 ▶ The following are examples of penicillins:

A = imipenem.	FALSE
B = aztreonam.	FALSE
C = flucloxacillin.	TRUE
D = vancomycin.	FALSE
E = methicillin.	TRUE

55 ▶ Metformin

A = is a sulphonylurea.	FALSE
B = lowers serum glucose.	FALSE
C = decreases the secretion of glucagon.	FALSE
D = is absorbed from the small intestine following oral intake.	TRUE
E = has a half-life of 2 hours.	TRUE

56 ▶ Lidocaine

A = is an ester of benzoic acid.	FALSE
B = is absorbed through intact skin.	TRUE
C = is dealkylated in the liver.	TRUE
D = must always be administered with a vasoconstrictor.	FALSE
E = may lead to coma if used in excess.	TRUE

57 ▶ The following are examples of aminoglycosides:

A = penicillamine.	FALSE
B = gentamicin.	TRUE
C = streptomycin.	TRUE
D = actinomycin D.	FALSE
E = amoxicillin.	FALSE

58 ▶ The following antibiotics contain a β-lactam ring:

A = penicillin G. TRUE

B = penicillin V. TRUE

C = clindamycin. FALSE

D = cephradine. TRUE

E = cefuroxime. TRUE

59 ▶ Trastuzumab

A = is an aromatase inhibitor. FALSE

B = should be taken orally. FALSE

C = may be used in the adjuvant treatment of breast cancer which over-expresses human epidermal growth factor receptor-2. TRUE

D = is cardiotoxic. TRUE

E = is capable of inducing apoptosis. TRUE

60 ▶ The two-sample unpaired t-test

A = is a non-parametric test. FALSE

B = compares two independent samples from the same population. TRUE

C = may be used in a study to compare maternal weight at delivery with paternal weight at delivery. TRUE

D = may be used in a study to compare tumour volume before and after chemotherapy. FALSE

E = is an example of a method of carrying out two-way analysis of variance by ranks. FALSE

61 ▶ Regression by least squares method

A = can be applied to measurements with a normal distribution. TRUE

B = applies to quantitative variables. TRUE

C = analyses two variables and allows one variable to be predicted from the other. TRUE

D = can be used to determine whether birth weight can be predicted from maternal calorific intake. TRUE

E = can be used to predict whether or not shoulder dystocia can be predicted from maternal calorific intake. FALSE

62 ▶ When comparing two groups,

A = the odds ratio is a method of representing probability. TRUE

B = the relative risk is a summary measure of the ratio of the risk of an actual event. TRUE

C = for a very rare event the odds ratio and the relative risk will be similar. TRUE

D = a high *P* value is strong evidence against the null hypothesis. FALSE

E = wide confidence intervals are preferable to narrow confidence intervals. FALSE

63 ▶ A study of birth weight was carried out among immigrant women from South East Asia living in an inner city area. The women had uncomplicated pregnancies and the birth weights of 10,000 babies were reliably measured. The results showed a perfect Gaussian distribution with a mean birth weight of 3050 grams and a standard deviation of 150 grams. The following statements are correct:

A = The median birth weight was 3050 grams. TRUE

B = The mode can be calculated by subtracting variance from mean. FALSE

C = Two-thirds of the babies had a birth weight between 2900 grams and 3200 grams. TRUE

D = 100 babies had a birth weight in excess of 3500 grams. FALSE

E = 6800 babies had a birth weight between 2900 grams and 3200 grams. TRUE

64 ▶ The Kruskall Wallis test

A = is an analysis of variance by ranks. TRUE

B = is a non-parametric test. TRUE

C = can be used in a study which examines four sets of observations on a single sample. TRUE

D = assesses the strength of the association between two continuous variables. FALSE

E = can be used in a study to determine whether intrauterine pressures are higher 1, 2 or 3 hours after forewater amniotomy at 40 weeks of gestation. TRUE

65 ▶ The following tests may be appropriately used in studies where the variables have a skewed distribution:

A = one-sample paired t-test. FALSE

B = two-sample unpaired t-test. FALSE

C = two-way analysis of variance by ranks. TRUE

D = F test. FALSE

E = Spearman's rank correlation coefficient. TRUE

66 ► A study reports that the mean systolic blood pressure in a certain treatment group was 100 mmHg with a 95% confidence interval between 95 mmHg and 105 mmHg. The following conclusions are valid:

A = We can be 95% confident that the true mean of that population lies between 95 mmHg and 105 mmHg.	TRUE
B = The interval between 95 mmHg and 105 mmHg has a 0.90 probability of containing the true population mean.	FALSE
C = The best estimate of the true population mean is 95 mmHg.	FALSE
D = The true population mean could possibly be less than 95 mmHg.	TRUE
E = The possibility that the true population mean is more than 110 mmHg is completely excluded.	FALSE

67 ► Evidence-based practice

A = is the process of systematically finding and using contemporaneous research findings as the basis for clinical decision making.	TRUE
B = relies on a maximum of 50% uptake of clinical guidelines.	FALSE
C = requires the formulation of clear clinical questions.	TRUE
D = requires the critical appraisal of the validity of a research report.	TRUE
E = requires the measurement of performance against expected outcomes.	TRUE

68 ▶ The following controls are entirely appropriate when there cannot be blinding for a clinical trial:

A = placebo.	TRUE
B = standard of care.	TRUE
C = historical. ✗	FALSE
D = blinded evaluator.	TRUE
E = objective endpoint.	TRUE

11 | Answers to full paper 2 (Chapter 5)

EMQ SECTION

1 ▶ *G* = 180.

2 ▶ *O* = 17,000.

3 ▶ *N* = Transferrin.

4 ▶ *B* = Decreased; Decreased; Normal.

5 ▶ *C* = Active antiport with potassium K^+.

6 ▶ *A* = 20–20,000 Hertz.

7 ▶ *E* = 3,000,000–7,500,000 Hertz.

8 ▶ *D* = Nucelotide; DNA.

9 ▶ *C* = Autosomal dominant; Neuromuscular degeneration from middle age onwards.

10 ▶ *L* = Autosomal recessive; Progressive incurable neurodegeneration in childhood.

11 ▶ *A* = Activation of the classical pathway.

12 ▶ *B* = Alcian blue.

13 ▶ *J* = Gram stain.

14 ▶ *E* = 90.

15 ▶ *B* = 44.

16 ▶ *D* = Goitre.

17 ▶ *C* = 25 g.

18 ▶ *I* = 1500 g.

19 ▶ *F* = Myeloblast; Phagocytosis; Yes; Yes.

20 ▶ *H* = Proerythroblast; Carriage of oxygen; No; No.

MCQ SECTION

21 ▶ Erythropoietin

A = is a polypeptide.	TRUE
B = initiates the synthesis of haemoglobin.	TRUE
C = is structurally related to erythromycin.	FALSE
D = may be isolated from the antrum of the stomach.	FALSE
E = is detectable in serum following bilateral nephrectomy.	TRUE

22 ▶ Ribosomal RNA

A = constitutes 60% of the ribosome.	TRUE
B = is synthesised in the nucleus.	TRUE
C = collects in the nucleolus.	TRUE
D = is absent in prokaryotic cells.	FALSE
E = is the catalytic component of the ribosome.	TRUE

23 ▶ The sodium–potassium pump

A = is an example of passive transport.	FALSE
B = transports potassium out of the cell under physiological conditions.	FALSE
C = requires adenosine triphosphate (ATP).	TRUE
D = is unique to nerve cells.	FALSE
E = is based around a carrier protein in the cell membrane.	TRUE

24 ▶ Oxytocin

A = is produced in the posterior lobe of the pituitary gland.	FALSE
B = is derived from the precursor for antidiuretic hormone.	FALSE
C = stimulates testosterone synthesis in the male.	TRUE
D = is released with neurophysin II as part of the suckling response in lactating females.	FALSE
E = binds to receptors on the myometrium.	TRUE

25 ▶ Nitric oxide mediates following physiological functions:

A = neurotransmission in the central nervous system.	TRUE
B = antibacterial activity of neutrophils.	TRUE
C = antiprotozoal activity of macrophages.	TRUE
D = platelet adhesiveness.	FALSE
E = contraction of cardiac muscle.	FALSE

26 ▶ The following hormones contain a cystine disulphide bridge:

A = antidiuretic hormone.	TRUE
B = oxytocin.	TRUE
C = growth hormone. + HPL	TRUE
D = aldosterone.	FALSE
E = testosterone.	FALSE

27 ▶ Human placental lactogen

A = is composed of two subunits – α and β. FALSE

B = stimulates lipolysis in adipose tissue. TRUE

C = is produced by the breasts. FALSE

D = is present at a much higher concentration in maternal blood than in the amniotic fluid. TRUE

E = enhances the transfer of amino acids across the placenta to the fetus. TRUE

28 ▶ The following molecules contain iron:

A = bilirubin. FALSE

B = biliverdin. FALSE

C = deoxygenated fetal haemoglobin. TRUE

D = haemoglobin S. TRUE

E = urobilinogen. FALSE

29 ▶ RNA polymerase

A = is template-dependent. TRUE

B = requires a primer. FALSE

C = binds to DNA promoter. TRUE

D = promotes the formation of mRNA without unwinding DNA. FALSE

E = is inhibited by rifampicin in mycobacterium tuberculosis. TRUE

30 ▶ Simple diffusion of a lipophilic solute across a plasma membrane

A = is affected by its diffusion coefficient.	TRUE
B = is unaffected by its concentration gradient.	FALSE
C = is energy-dependent.	FALSE
D = can be stopped by inhibition of Na^+, K^+ – ATPase.	FALSE
E = requires the simultaneous transport of a molecule of similar structure to travel in the opposite direction through the same channel.	FALSE

31 ▶ The Golgi complex is associated with the following functions:

A = synthesis of DNA.	FALSE
B = synthesis of RNA.	FALSE
C = synthesis of new membranes.	TRUE
D = formation of lysosomes.	TRUE
E = formation of peroxisomes.	TRUE

32 ▶ The resting membrane potential of nerve cells is

A = approximately +90 millivolts.	FALSE
B = determined mainly by the sodium–potassium membrane pump.	FALSE
C = affected by the permeability of the nerve cell membrane to sodium ions.	TRUE
D = affected by the diffusion of potassium ions.	TRUE
E = a prerequisite for the transmission of impulses.	TRUE

33 ▶ One Gray is

A = the absorbed dose of radiation per kilogram.	TRUE
B = measured in joules per kilogram.	TRUE
C = equivalent to 1000 rad.	FALSE
D = expected to produce a rise in temperature of 10°c per kilogram.	FALSE
E = also used to measure radiation in obstetric ultrasound.	FALSE

34 ▶ The following types of ionising radiation have high linear energy transfer (LET):

A = neutron beam.	TRUE
B = alpha particles.	TRUE
C = heavy ions.	TRUE
D = X-rays.	FALSE
E = γ-rays.	FALSE

35 ▶ The effects of radiotherapy on a tumour are

A = increased by hypoxia.	FALSE
B = usually increased by an inadequate blood supply, which results in hypoxia.	FALSE
C = are increased by oxygenation.	TRUE
D = dependent on the radiosensitivity of the tumour.	TRUE
E = due to damage of the DNA in the cells.	TRUE

36 ▶ Radiation-induced damage to the cell includes

A = double-strand break of DNA. TRUE

B = single strand break of DNA. TRUE

C = formation of intrastrand crosslinks within DNA. TRUE

D = formation of DNA interstrand crosslinks. TRUE

E = formation of crosslinks between DNA and nuclear proteins. TRUE

37 ▶ DNA contains

A = 2-deoxy-D-ribose. TRUE

B = phosphate esters. TRUE

C = uracil. FALSE

D = uridine. FALSE

E = deoxythymidine. TRUE

38 ▶ The following are examples of conditions where both alleles must be mutated to cause the disease:

A = Tay Sachs disease. TRUE

B = congenital adrenal hyperplasia. TRUE

C = Vitamin D-resistant rickets. FALSE

D = haemophilia A. FALSE

E = Edwards syndrome. FALSE

39 ▶ A woman who is a gene carrier for cystic fibrosis marries a man who is also a gene carrier for cystic fibrosis. The risks to their offspring can be stated as follows:

A = The risk of an affected child is one in four.	TRUE
B = The risk of an affected son is one in four.	FALSE
C = The risk of an affected daughter is one in four.	FALSE
D = The risk of a child who is a carrier is greater than the gene frequency of the condition in a North European population.	TRUE
E = If the couple have an affected son, then the risk to the child in the next pregnancy of having the condition is one in eight.	FALSE

40 ▶ The following are examples of single gene disorders with an autosomal dominant type of inheritance:

A = myotonic dystrophy.	TRUE
B = Duchenne muscular dystrophy.	FALSE
C = anencephaly.	FALSE
D = Xg blood group.	FALSE
E = erythaema multiforme.	FALSE

41 ▶ The following conditions are inherited as an autosomal recessive:

A = congenital adrenal hyperplasia due to 21-hydroxylase deficiency.	TRUE
B = glucose-6-phosphate dehydrogenase deficiency.	FALSE
C = nephrogenic diabetes insipidus.	FALSE
D = congenital talipes equino varus.	FALSE
E = β-thalassaemia.	TRUE

42 ▶ The following conditions are inherited as a X-linked dominant:

A = achondroplasia.	FALSE
B = 47,XXX.	FALSE
C = 47,XXY.	FALSE
D = fragile X syndrome.	FALSE
E = holoprosencephaly.	FALSE

43 ▶ The following are examples of single gene disorders with X-linked inheritance:

A = galactosaemia.	FALSE
B = glucose-6-phosphate dehydrogenase deficiency.	TRUE
C = vitamin D resistant rickets.	TRUE
D = Lesch–Nyhan syndrome.	TRUE
E = cutaneous lichen sclerosus (CREST syndrome).	FALSE

44 ▶ The following steps are necessary for the processing of pre-mRNA to mRNA:

A = binding with small nuclear ribonucleoproteins.	TRUE
B = removal of introns.	TRUE
C = joining of exons.	TRUE
D = polyadenylation.	TRUE
E = topoisomerisation.	FALSE

45 ▶ Tetanus

A = is caused by the release of an endotoxin.	FALSE
B = may result from infection of the umbilical stump of the newborn.	TRUE
C = leads to flaccid paralysis.	FALSE
D = is effectively prevented by using an attenuated vaccine prepared from the causative organism.	FALSE
E = is associated with overactivity of the sympathetic nervous system.	TRUE

46 ▶ Vaccines are available against:

A = tuberculosis.	TRUE
B = syphilis.	FALSE
C = gonorrhoea.	FALSE
D = tetanus.	TRUE
E = diphtheria.	TRUE

47 ▶ The BCG vaccine

A = induces cell-mediated immunity.	TRUE
B = is an example of an attenuated bacterial vaccine.	TRUE
C = contains mycobacteria that often revert to virulence.	FALSE
D = must never be given to an infant aged less than 6 months.	FALSE
E = is effective at preventing tubercular meningitis.	TRUE

48 ▶ Wound healing is promoted by

A = hypoxia.	FALSE
B = bacterial infection.	FALSE
C = corticosteroids.	FALSE
D = platelet degranulation.	TRUE
E = myofibroblasts.	TRUE

49 ▶ In cases of postmortem following maternal mortality, blocks for histological examination must be taken from the following organs as a minimum:

A = spleen.	FALSE
B = femur.	FALSE
C = kidney.	TRUE
D = brain.	TRUE
E = supraclavicular lymph nodes.	FALSE

50 ▶ Creatinine clearance

A = may be calculated from measurement of serum creatinine and the concentration of urinary creatinine.	FALSE
B = is approximately 120 ml/minute in the healthy adult.	TRUE
C = may be elevated to 190 ml/minute in a pregnant woman with diabetes who is taking insulin.	TRUE
D = is an approximate measure of the glomerular filtration rate.	TRUE
E = may be markedly elevated in the initial phase of acute renal failure.	FALSE

51 ▶ Primary syphilis

A = appears as a painless genital ulcer within 1 week of infection. FALSE

B = produces well-defined and indurated lesions. TRUE

C = produces lesions before seroconversion. FALSE

D = produces lesions in the genital area only. FALSE

E = is followed by a period of asymptomatic latency. TRUE

52 ▶ The following conditions are premalignant:

A = balanitis xerotica obliterans. FALSE

B = syphilitic chancre. FALSE

C = xeroderma pigmentosum. TRUE

D = Paget's disease of bone. TRUE

E = ulcerative colitis. TRUE

53 ▶ Examples of carcinogens include:

A = ionising radiation. TRUE

B = 3,4-benzpyrene. TRUE

C = β-naphthylamine. TRUE

D = oxytocin. FALSE

E = ergotamine. FALSE

54 ▶ Characteristics of a malignant neoplasm include:

A = resemblance to tissue of origin.	FALSE
B = well-circumscribed border.	FALSE
C = necrotic areas.	TRUE
D = invasion of surrounding tissues.	TRUE
E = normal nuclear morphology.	FALSE

55 ▶ The following are examples of tumours of epithelial origin:

A = melanoma.	FALSE
B = adenocarcinoma.	TRUE
C = squamous carcinoma.	TRUE
D = hepatoblastoma.	FALSE
E = rhabdomyosarcoma.	FALSE

56 ▶ The following are examples of tumours of mesenchymal origin:

A = osteoma.	TRUE
B = chondroma.	TRUE
C = lipoma.	TRUE
D = neurofibroma.	TRUE
E = squamous papilloma.	FALSE

57 ▶ The following conditions are uniformly lethal:

A = anencephaly.	TRUE
B = Down syndrome.	FALSE
C = Edwards syndrome.	TRUE
D = Patau syndrome.	TRUE
E = β-thalassaemia trait.	FALSE

58 ▶ Gonorrhoea is a cause of

A = epididymitis.	TRUE
B = endocarditis.	TRUE
C = encephalitis.	FALSE
D = gummatous necrosis of the liver.	FALSE
E = cutaneous lesions.	TRUE

59 ▶ Visceral Leishmaniasis

A = is caused by *Leishmania donovani*.	TRUE
B = depends on the mosquito to act as a vector.	FALSE
C = is a cause of massive splenomegaly.	TRUE
D = may lead to liver failure if untreated.	TRUE
E = is treated by aminoglycosides.	FALSE

60 ▶ Normal bile contains the following:

A = cholesterol.	TRUE
B = bilirubin.	TRUE
C = biliverdin.	FALSE
D = stercobilin.	FALSE
E = urobilin.	FALSE

61 ▶ In the normal adult's electrocardiogram, the

A = P wave represents the pressure in the right atrium.	FALSE
B = QRS complex represents ventricular depolarisation.	TRUE
C = PR interval varies between 1 and 2 seconds.	FALSE
D = ST segment represents atrial repolarisation.	FALSE
E = T wave represents ventricular repolarisation.	TRUE

62 ▶ A healthy pregnant woman travels by helicopter from sea level to an altitude of 4000 metres. The physiological changes which would be evident within 30 minutes include

A = increased alveolar ventilation rate.	TRUE
B = increased pulmonary blood flow.	TRUE
C = hypercapnia.	FALSE
D = fall in arterial pH.	FALSE
E = increased vascularity of peripheral tissues.	FALSE

63 ▶ Growth hormone secretion is increased by

A = kwashiorkor.	TRUE
B = testosterone.	TRUE
C = estradiol.	TRUE
D = somatostatin.	FALSE
E = increased level of free fatty acids in the blood.	FALSE

64 ▶ Aldosterone

A = is an example of a steroid hormone.	TRUE
B = contains 21 carbon atoms in each molecule.	TRUE
C = is derived from Δ^5 pregnenolone.	TRUE
D = is synthesised in the cells of the zona fasciculata of the adrenal cortex.	FALSE
E = synthesis is inhibited by acetylcholine.	FALSE

65 ▶ During normal pregnancy in a healthy woman, the anterior pituitary gland

A = decreases in size.	FALSE
B = secretes significantly less follicle-stimulating hormone (FSH).	TRUE
C = secretes significantly less luteinising hormone (LH).	TRUE
D = increases secretion of prolactin.	TRUE
E = secretes less adrenocorticotrophic hormone (ACTH).	FALSE

66 ▶ The concentration of the following substances is higher in fetal blood than in maternal blood in a normal pregnancy in a healthy woman:

A = riboflavin	TRUE
B = vitamin B_{12}.	TRUE
C = oxygen.	TRUE
D = calcium.	TRUE
E = basic amino acids.	TRUE

67 ▶ Renin

A = is an enzyme.	TRUE
B = catalyses the reaction to convert angiotensinogen to angiotensin 1.	TRUE
C = is synthesised by hepatocytes.	FALSE
D = release is inhibited by nonsteroidal anti-inflammatory drugs.	TRUE
E = release is stimulated by adenosine.	FALSE

68 ▶ In a healthy supine woman, the mean pulmonary arterial pressure is higher than the mean pressure in the following:

A = superior vena cava.	TRUE
B = pulmonary veins.	TRUE
C = uterine artery.	FALSE
D = left atrium.	TRUE
E = aortic arch.	FALSE

12 | Answers to standalone EMQ paper 1 (Chapter 6)

OPTIONS

1 ▶ *A* = Abdominal aorta.

2 ▶ *F* = Internal iliac artery.

3 ▶ *E* = Right ovarian artery, branch of the abdominal aorta; Right ovarian vein leading to the inferior vena cava; By the corpus luteum during the luteal phase.

4 ▶ *C* = Ureteric bud from the mesonephric duct; Renal sinus to the base of the urinary bladder.

5 ▶ *G* =13%.

6 ▶ *K* = 0.5%.

7 ▶ *F* = RNA; Yes; Available.

8 ▶ *A* = DNA; No; Available.

9 ▶ *O* = *Treponema pallidum* subspecies endemicum.

10 ▶ *E* = Day 25.

11 ▶ *G* = Day 33.

12 ▶ *B* = 1.

13 ▶ *F* = 5.

14 ▶ *H* = Beta cells; Liver, skeletal muscle, adipose tissue; Lowered.

15 ▶ *E* = Induction of cytochrome P450.

16 ▶ *G* = Inhibition of bacterial wall synthesis.

17 ▶ *K* = Inhibition of retroviral nucleoside reverse transcriptase.

18 ▶ $B = 10$.

19 ▶ I = Renal peritubular endothelial cells; Initiation of multiple signalling pathways in erythrocyte precursors.

20 ▶ $E = 0.05$.

13 | Answers to standalone EMQ paper 2 (Chapter 7)

OPTIONS

1 ▶ *F* = 280.

2 ▶ *D* = Respiratory alkalosis.

3 ▶ *A* = Metabolic acidosis.

4 ▶ *A* = Early embryonic development.

5 ▶ *F* = Puberty.

6 ▶ *F* = Neuropathy.

7 ▶ *A* = Cardiomyopathy.

8 ▶ *C* = Breast cancer and ovarian cancer.

9 ▶ *E* = Breast cancer, brain tumours, adrenocortical cancer, leukaemia, sarcoma of bone and soft tissue.

10 ▶ *L* = Chromosome 16.

11 ▶ *D* = Immunoglobulin G (IgG).

12 ▶ *C* = Cystic fibrosis.

13 ▶ *O* = Periodic Acid Schiff.

14 ▶ *N* = Masson-Fontana.

15 ▶ *F* = Autosomal recessive; Hexosaminidase A.

16 ▶ *H* = Autosomal recessive; Sphingomyelinase.

17 ▶ *B* = Increased; Decreased.

18 ▶ *D* = Decreased; Decreased.

19 ▶ $H = 140$.

20 ▶ $A = 7$.

14 | Answers to standalone EMQ paper 3 (Chapter 8)

OPTIONS

1 ▶ *H* = Superior vena cava and inferior vena cava; Superior vena cava and inferior vena cava.

2 ▶ *C* = Four pulmonary veins; Right ventricle.

3 ▶ *C* = Ureteric bud from the mesonephric duct; Renal sinus to the base of the urinary bladder.

4 ▶ *B* = Left ovarian artery, branch of the abdominal aorta; Left ovarian vein leading to the left renal vein; By the corpus luteum during the luteal phase.

5 ▶ *B* = Endoderm epithelium.

6 ▶ *C* = Mesenchyme.

7 ▶ *I* = 300.

8 ▶ *D* = 5.

9 ▶ *I* = Islets of Langerhans in the pancreas.

10 ▶ *C* = Anterior lobe of the pituitary gland.

11 ▶ *N* = *Treponema carateum*.

12 ▶ *G* = Inhibition of bacterial wall synthesis.

13 ▶ *Q* = Schizonticidal within hepatocytes.

14 ▶ *E* = Anti-estrogen.

15 ▶ *N* = Tocolytic.

16 ▶ *J* = Progestogen.

17 ▶ $C = 1$.

18 ▶ $G = 90$.

19 ▶ $B = 3$ mmHg.

20 ▶ $G = 8$ mmHg.

15 | Answers to standalone EMQ paper 4 (Chapter 9)

OPTIONS

1 ▶ *E* = Produced as a result of the action of biliverdin reductase on biliverdin; Albumin; 450 nm.

2 ▶ *A* = Activation of plasminogen to plasmin.

3 ▶ *E* = Inactivation of free plasmin.

4 ▶ *D* = Channel-mediated diffusion.

5 ▶ *B* = ATP-mediated diffusion.

6 ▶ *J* = 16,000.

7 ▶ *L* = 22,000.

8 ▶ *E* = Autosomal recessive; Glucose-6-phosphatase.

9 ▶ *N* = X-linked recessive; Iduronate sulphatase.

10 ▶ *F* = Nucleotide; RNA.

11 ▶ *A* = Immunoglobulin A (IgA).

12 ▶ *A* = Acrodermatitis enteropathica.

13 ▶ *H* = Congo red.

14 ▶ *J* = Gram stain.

15 ▶ *P* = 200.

16 ▶ *C* = 70.

17 ▶ *B* = Duodenum and jejunum.

18 ▶ *A* = Colon.

19 ▶ *I* = Myoglobin.

20 ▶ *B* = Caeruloplasmin.

Appendix 1
Quick reference answer keys

Please use these to quickly mark your self-testing efforts.

Full mock examination paper I (paper I type – Chapter 4)

EMQ SECTION

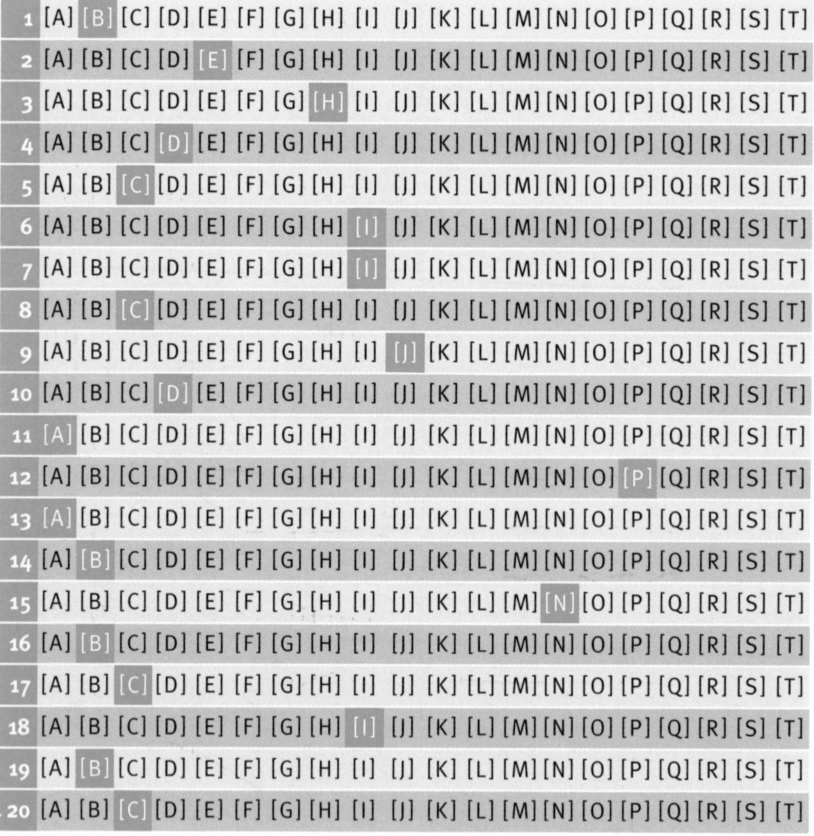

1	[A]	**[B]**	[C]	[D]	[E]	[F]	[G]	[H]	[I]	[J]	[K]	[L]	[M]	[N]	[O]	[P]	[Q]	[R]	[S]	[T]
2	[A]	[B]	[C]	[D]	**[E]**	[F]	[G]	[H]	[I]	[J]	[K]	[L]	[M]	[N]	[O]	[P]	[Q]	[R]	[S]	[T]
3	[A]	[B]	[C]	[D]	[E]	[F]	[G]	**[H]**	[I]	[J]	[K]	[L]	[M]	[N]	[O]	[P]	[Q]	[R]	[S]	[T]
4	[A]	[B]	[C]	**[D]**	[E]	[F]	[G]	[H]	[I]	[J]	[K]	[L]	[M]	[N]	[O]	[P]	[Q]	[R]	[S]	[T]
5	[A]	[B]	**[C]**	[D]	[E]	[F]	[G]	[H]	[I]	[J]	[K]	[L]	[M]	[N]	[O]	[P]	[Q]	[R]	[S]	[T]
6	[A]	[B]	[C]	[D]	[E]	[F]	[G]	[H]	**[I]**	[J]	[K]	[L]	[M]	[N]	[O]	[P]	[Q]	[R]	[S]	[T]
7	[A]	[B]	[C]	[D]	[E]	[F]	[G]	[H]	**[I]**	[J]	[K]	[L]	[M]	[N]	[O]	[P]	[Q]	[R]	[S]	[T]
8	[A]	[B]	**[C]**	[D]	[E]	[F]	[G]	[H]	[I]	[J]	[K]	[L]	[M]	[N]	[O]	[P]	[Q]	[R]	[S]	[T]
9	[A]	[B]	[C]	[D]	[E]	[F]	[G]	[H]	[I]	**[J]**	[K]	[L]	[M]	[N]	[O]	[P]	[Q]	[R]	[S]	[T]
10	[A]	[B]	[C]	**[D]**	[E]	[F]	[G]	[H]	[I]	[J]	[K]	[L]	[M]	[N]	[O]	[P]	[Q]	[R]	[S]	[T]
11	**[A]**	[B]	[C]	[D]	[E]	[F]	[G]	[H]	[I]	[J]	[K]	[L]	[M]	[N]	[O]	[P]	[Q]	[R]	[S]	[T]
12	[A]	[B]	[C]	[D]	[E]	[F]	[G]	[H]	[I]	[J]	[K]	[L]	[M]	[N]	[O]	**[P]**	[Q]	[R]	[S]	[T]
13	**[A]**	[B]	[C]	[D]	[E]	[F]	[G]	[H]	[I]	[J]	[K]	[L]	[M]	[N]	[O]	[P]	[Q]	[R]	[S]	[T]
14	[A]	**[B]**	[C]	[D]	[E]	[F]	[G]	[H]	[I]	[J]	[K]	[L]	[M]	[N]	[O]	[P]	[Q]	[R]	[S]	[T]
15	[A]	[B]	[C]	[D]	[E]	[F]	[G]	[H]	[I]	[J]	[K]	[L]	[M]	**[N]**	[O]	[P]	[Q]	[R]	[S]	[T]
16	[A]	**[B]**	[C]	[D]	[E]	[F]	[G]	[H]	[I]	[J]	[K]	[L]	[M]	[N]	[O]	[P]	[Q]	[R]	[S]	[T]
17	[A]	[B]	**[C]**	[D]	[E]	[F]	[G]	[H]	[I]	[J]	[K]	[L]	[M]	[N]	[O]	[P]	[Q]	[R]	[S]	[T]
18	[A]	[B]	[C]	[D]	[E]	[F]	[G]	[H]	**[I]**	[J]	[K]	[L]	[M]	[N]	[O]	[P]	[Q]	[R]	[S]	[T]
19	[A]	**[B]**	[C]	[D]	[E]	[F]	[G]	[H]	[I]	[J]	[K]	[L]	[M]	[N]	[O]	[P]	[Q]	[R]	[S]	[T]
20	[A]	[B]	**[C]**	[D]	[E]	[F]	[G]	[H]	[I]	[J]	[K]	[L]	[M]	[N]	[O]	[P]	[Q]	[R]	[S]	[T]

MCQ SECTION

	A	B	C	D	E
21	[T]	[T]	[T]	[T]	[T]
	[F]	[F]	[F]	[F]	[F]
22	[T]	[T]	[T]	[T]	[T]
	[F]	[F]	[F]	[F]	[F]
23	[T]	[T]	[T]	[T]	[T]
	[F]	[F]	[F]	[F]	[F]
24	[T]	[T]	[T]	[T]	[T]
	[F]	[F]	[F]	[F]	[F]
25	[T]	[T]	[T]	[T]	[T]
	[F]	[F]	[F]	[F]	[F]
26	[T]	[T]	[T]	[T]	[T]
	[F]	[F]	[F]	[F]	[F]
27	[T]	[T]	[T]	[T]	[T]
	[F]	[F]	[F]	[F]	[F]
28	[T]	[T]	[T]	[T]	[T]
	[F]	[F]	[F]	[F]	[F]
29	[T]	[T]	[T]	[T]	[T]
	[F]	[F]	[F]	[F]	[F]
30	[T]	[T]	[T]	[T]	[T]
	[F]	[F]	[F]	[F]	[F]
31	[T]	[T]	[T]	[T]	[T]
	[F]	[F]	[F]	[F]	[F]
32	[T]	[T]	[T]	[T]	[T]
	[F]	[F]	[F]	[F]	[F]
33	[T]	[T]	[T]	[T]	[T]
	[F]	[F]	[F]	[F]	[F]
34	[T]	[T]	[T]	[T]	[T]
	[F]	[F]	[F]	[F]	[F]
35	[T]	[T]	[T]	[T]	[T]
	[F]	[F]	[F]	[F]	[F]
36	[T]	[T]	[T]	[T]	[T]
	[F]	[F]	[F]	[F]	[F]

	A	B	C	D	E
37	[T]	[T]	[T]	[T]	[T]
	[F]	[F]	[F]	[F]	[F]
38	[T]	[T]	[T]	[T]	[T]
	[F]	[F]	[F]	[F]	[F]
39	[T]	[T]	[T]	[T]	[T]
	[F]	[F]	[F]	[F]	[F]
40	[T]	[T]	[T]	[T]	[T]
	[F]	[F]	[F]	[F]	[F]
41	[T]	[T]	[T]	[T]	[T]
	[F]	[F]	[F]	[F]	[F]
42	[T]	[T]	[T]	[T]	[T]
	[F]	[F]	[F]	[F]	[F]
43	[T]	[T]	[T]	[T]	[T]
	[F]	[F]	[F]	[F]	[F]
44	[T]	[T]	[T]	[T]	[T]
	[F]	[F]	[F]	[F]	[F]
45	[T]	[T]	[T]	[T]	[T]
	[F]	[F]	[F]	[F]	[F]
46	[T]	[T]	[T]	[T]	[T]
	[F]	[F]	[F]	[F]	[F]
47	[T]	[T]	[T]	[T]	[T]
	[F]	[F]	[F]	[F]	[F]
48	[T]	[T]	[T]	[T]	[T]
	[F]	[F]	[F]	[F]	[F]
49	[T]	[T]	[T]	[T]	[T]
	[F]	[F]	[F]	[F]	[F]
50	[T]	[T]	[T]	[T]	[T]
	[F]	[F]	[F]	[F]	[F]
51	[T]	[T]	[T]	[T]	[T]
	[F]	[F]	[F]	[F]	[F]
52	[T]	[T]	[T]	[T]	[T]
	[F]	[F]	[F]	[F]	[F]

	A	B	C	D	E
53	[T]	[T]	[T]	[T]	[T]
	[F]	[F]	[F]	[F]	[F]
54	[T]	[T]	[T]	[T]	[T]
	[F]	[F]	[F]	[F]	[F]
55	[T]	[T]	[T]	[T]	[T]
	[F]	[F]	[F]	[F]	[F]
56	[T]	[T]	[T]	[T]	[T]
	[F]	[F]	[F]	[F]	[F]
57	[T]	[T]	[T]	[T]	[T]
	[F]	[F]	[F]	[F]	[F]
58	[T]	[T]	[T]	[T]	[T]
	[F]	[F]	[F]	[F]	[F]
59	[T]	[T]	[T]	[T]	[T]
	[F]	[F]	[F]	[F]	[F]
60	[T]	[T]	[T]	[T]	[T]
	[F]	[F]	[F]	[F]	[F]
61	[T]	[T]	[T]	[T]	[T]
	[F]	[F]	[F]	[F]	[F]
62	[T]	[T]	[T]	[T]	[T]
	[F]	[F]	[F]	[F]	[F]
63	[T]	[T]	[T]	[T]	[T]
	[F]	[F]	[F]	[F]	[F]
64	[T]	[T]	[T]	[T]	[T]
	[F]	[F]	[F]	[F]	[F]
65	[T]	[T]	[T]	[T]	[T]
	[F]	[F]	[F]	[F]	[F]
66	[T]	[T]	[T]	[T]	[T]
	[F]	[F]	[F]	[F]	[F]
67	[T]	[T]	[T]	[T]	[T]
	[F]	[F]	[F]	[F]	[F]
68	[T]	[T]	[T]	[T]	[T]
	[F]	[F]	[F]	[F]	[F]

Full mock examination paper 2 (paper 2 type – Chapter 5)

EMQ SECTION

1	[A]	[B]	[C]	[D]	[E]	[F]	**[G]**	[H]	[I]	[J]	[K]	[L]	[M]	[N]	[O]	[P]	[Q]	[R]	[S]	[T]
2	[A]	[B]	[C]	[D]	[E]	[F]	[G]	[H]	[I]	[J]	[K]	[L]	[M]	[N]	**[O]**	[P]	[Q]	[R]	[S]	[T]
3	[A]	[B]	[C]	[D]	[E]	[F]	[G]	[H]	[I]	[J]	[K]	[L]	[M]	**[N]**	[O]	[P]	[Q]	[R]	[S]	[T]
4	[A]	**[B]**	[C]	[D]	[E]	[F]	[G]	[H]	[I]	[J]	[K]	[L]	[M]	[N]	[O]	[P]	[Q]	[R]	[S]	[T]
5	[A]	[B]	**[C]**	[D]	[E]	[F]	[G]	[H]	[I]	[J]	[K]	[L]	[M]	[N]	[O]	[P]	[Q]	[R]	[S]	[T]
6	**[A]**	[B]	[C]	[D]	[E]	[F]	[G]	[H]	[I]	[J]	[K]	[L]	[M]	[N]	[O]	[P]	[Q]	[R]	[S]	[T]
7	[A]	[B]	[C]	[D]	**[E]**	[F]	[G]	[H]	[I]	[J]	[K]	[L]	[M]	[N]	[O]	[P]	[Q]	[R]	[S]	[T]
8	[A]	[B]	[C]	**[D]**	[E]	[F]	[G]	[H]	[I]	[J]	[K]	[L]	[M]	[N]	[O]	[P]	[Q]	[R]	[S]	[T]
9	[A]	[B]	**[C]**	[D]	[E]	[F]	[G]	[H]	[I]	[J]	[K]	[L]	[M]	[N]	[O]	[P]	[Q]	[R]	[S]	[T]
10	[A]	[B]	[C]	[D]	[E]	[F]	[G]	[H]	[I]	[J]	[K]	**[L]**	[M]	[N]	[O]	[P]	[Q]	[R]	[S]	[T]
11	**[A]**	[B]	[C]	[D]	[E]	[F]	[G]	[H]	[I]	[J]	[K]	[L]	[M]	[N]	[O]	[P]	[Q]	[R]	[S]	[T]
12	[A]	**[B]**	[C]	[D]	[E]	[F]	[G]	[H]	[I]	[J]	[K]	[L]	[M]	[N]	[O]	[P]	[Q]	[R]	[S]	[T]
13	[A]	[B]	[C]	[D]	[E]	[F]	[G]	[H]	[I]	**[J]**	[K]	[L]	[M]	[N]	[O]	[P]	[Q]	[R]	[S]	[T]
14	[A]	[B]	[C]	[D]	**[E]**	[F]	[G]	[H]	[I]	[J]	[K]	[L]	[M]	[N]	[O]	[P]	[Q]	[R]	[S]	[T]
15	[A]	**[B]**	[C]	[D]	[E]	[F]	[G]	[H]	[I]	[J]	[K]	[L]	[M]	[N]	[O]	[P]	[Q]	[R]	[S]	[T]
16	[A]	[B]	[C]	**[D]**	[E]	[F]	[G]	[H]	[I]	[J]	[K]	[L]	[M]	[N]	[O]	[P]	[Q]	[R]	[S]	[T]
17	[A]	[B]	**[C]**	[D]	[E]	[F]	[G]	[H]	[I]	[J]	[K]	[L]	[M]	[N]	[O]	[P]	[Q]	[R]	[S]	[T]
18	[A]	[B]	[C]	[D]	[E]	[F]	[G]	[H]	**[I]**	[J]	[K]	[L]	[M]	[N]	[O]	[P]	[Q]	[R]	[S]	[T]
19	[A]	[B]	[C]	[D]	[E]	**[F]**	[G]	[H]	[I]	[J]	[K]	[L]	[M]	[N]	[O]	[P]	[Q]	[R]	[S]	[T]
20	[A]	[B]	[C]	[D]	[E]	[F]	[G]	**[H]**	[I]	[J]	[K]	[L]	[M]	[N]	[O]	[P]	[Q]	[R]	[S]	[T]

MCQ SECTION

	A	B	C	D	E
21	[T]	[T]	[T]	[T]	[T]
	[F]	[F]	[F]	[F]	[F]
22	[T]	[T]	[T]	[T]	[T]
	[F]	[F]	[F]	[F]	[F]
23	[T]	[T]	[T]	[T]	[T]
	[F]	[F]	[F]	[F]	[F]
24	[T]	[T]	[T]	[T]	[T]
	[F]	[F]	[F]	[F]	[F]
25	[T]	[T]	[T]	[T]	[T]
	[F]	[F]	[F]	[F]	[F]
26	[T]	[T]	[T]	[T]	[T]
	[F]	[F]	[F]	[F]	[F]
27	[T]	[T]	[T]	[T]	[T]
	[F]	[F]	[F]	[F]	[F]
28	[T]	[T]	[T]	[T]	[T]
	[F]	[F]	[F]	[F]	[F]
29	[T]	[T]	[T]	[T]	[T]
	[F]	[F]	[F]	[F]	[F]
30	[T]	[T]	[T]	[T]	[T]
	[F]	[F]	[F]	[F]	[F]
31	[T]	[T]	[T]	[T]	[T]
	[F]	[F]	[F]	[F]	[F]
32	[T]	[T]	[T]	[T]	[T]
	[F]	[F]	[F]	[F]	[F]
33	[T]	[T]	[T]	[T]	[T]
	[F]	[F]	[F]	[F]	[F]
34	[T]	[T]	[T]	[T]	[T]
	[F]	[F]	[F]	[F]	[F]
35	[T]	[T]	[T]	[T]	[T]
	[F]	[F]	[F]	[F]	[F]
36	[T]	[T]	[T]	[T]	[T]
	[F]	[F]	[F]	[F]	[F]

	A	B	C	D	E
37	[T]	[T]	[T]	[T]	[T]
	[F]	[F]	[F]	[F]	[F]
38	[T]	[T]	[T]	[T]	[T]
	[F]	[F]	[F]	[F]	[F]
39	[T]	[T]	[T]	[T]	[T]
	[F]	[F]	[F]	[F]	[F]
40	[T]	[T]	[T]	[T]	[T]
	[F]	[F]	[F]	[F]	[F]
41	[T]	[T]	[T]	[T]	[T]
	[F]	[F]	[F]	[F]	[F]
42	[T]	[T]	[T]	[T]	[T]
	[F]	[F]	[F]	[F]	[F]
43	[T]	[T]	[T]	[T]	[T]
	[F]	[F]	[F]	[F]	[F]
44	[T]	[T]	[T]	[T]	[T]
	[F]	[F]	[F]	[F]	[F]
45	[T]	[T]	[T]	[T]	[T]
	[F]	[F]	[F]	[F]	[F]
46	[T]	[T]	[T]	[T]	[T]
	[F]	[F]	[F]	[F]	[F]
47	[T]	[T]	[T]	[T]	[T]
	[F]	[F]	[F]	[F]	[F]
48	[T]	[T]	[T]	[T]	[T]
	[F]	[F]	[F]	[F]	[F]
49	[T]	[T]	[T]	[T]	[T]
	[F]	[F]	[F]	[F]	[F]
50	[T]	[T]	[T]	[T]	[T]
	[F]	[F]	[F]	[F]	[F]
51	[T]	[T]	[T]	[T]	[T]
	[F]	[F]	[F]	[F]	[F]
52	[T]	[T]	[T]	[T]	[T]
	[F]	[F]	[F]	[F]	[F]

	A	B	C	D	E
53	[T]	[T]	[T]	[T]	[T]
	[F]	[F]	[F]	[F]	[F]
54	[T]	[T]	[T]	[T]	[T]
	[F]	[F]	[F]	[F]	[F]
55	[T]	[T]	[T]	[T]	[T]
	[F]	[F]	[F]	[F]	[F]
56	[T]	[T]	[T]	[T]	[T]
	[F]	[F]	[F]	[F]	[F]
57	[T]	[T]	[T]	[T]	[T]
	[F]	[F]	[F]	[F]	[F]
58	[T]	[T]	[T]	[T]	[T]
	[F]	[F]	[F]	[F]	[F]
59	[T]	[T]	[T]	[T]	[T]
	[F]	[F]	[F]	[F]	[F]
60	[T]	[T]	[T]	[T]	[T]
	[F]	[F]	[F]	[F]	[F]
61	[T]	[T]	[T]	[T]	[T]
	[F]	[F]	[F]	[F]	[F]
62	[T]	[T]	[T]	[T]	[T]
	[F]	[F]	[F]	[F]	[F]
63	[T]	[T]	[T]	[T]	[T]
	[F]	[F]	[F]	[F]	[F]
64	[T]	[T]	[T]	[T]	[T]
	[F]	[F]	[F]	[F]	[F]
65	[T]	[T]	[T]	[T]	[T]
	[F]	[F]	[F]	[F]	[F]
66	[T]	[T]	[T]	[T]	[T]
	[F]	[F]	[F]	[F]	[F]
67	[T]	[T]	[T]	[T]	[T]
	[F]	[F]	[F]	[F]	[F]
68	[T]	[T]	[T]	[T]	[T]
	[F]	[F]	[F]	[F]	[F]

Standalone EMQ paper 1 (paper 1 type – Chapter 6)

1	**[A]**	[B]	[C]	[D]	[E]	[F]	[G]	[H]	[I]	[J]	[K]	[L]	[M]	[N]	[O]	[P]	[Q]	[R]	[S]	[T]
2	[A]	[B]	[C]	[D]	[E]	**[F]**	[G]	[H]	[I]	[J]	[K]	[L]	[M]	[N]	[O]	[P]	[Q]	[R]	[S]	[T]
3	[A]	[B]	[C]	[D]	**[E]**	[F]	[G]	[H]	[I]	[J]	[K]	[L]	[M]	[N]	[O]	[P]	[Q]	[R]	[S]	[T]
4	[A]	[B]	**[C]**	[D]	[E]	[F]	[G]	[H]	[I]	[J]	[K]	[L]	[M]	[N]	[O]	[P]	[Q]	[R]	[S]	[T]
5	[A]	[B]	[C]	[D]	[E]	[F]	**[G]**	[H]	[I]	[J]	[K]	[L]	[M]	[N]	[O]	[P]	[Q]	[R]	[S]	[T]
6	[A]	[B]	[C]	[D]	[E]	[F]	[G]	[H]	[I]	[J]	**[K]**	[L]	[M]	[N]	[O]	[P]	[Q]	[R]	[S]	[T]
7	[A]	[B]	[C]	[D]	[E]	**[F]**	[G]	[H]	[I]	[J]	[K]	[L]	[M]	[N]	[O]	[P]	[Q]	[R]	[S]	[T]
8	**[A]**	[B]	[C]	[D]	[E]	[F]	[G]	[H]	[I]	[J]	[K]	[L]	[M]	[N]	[O]	[P]	[Q]	[R]	[S]	[T]
9	[A]	[B]	[C]	[D]	[E]	[F]	[G]	[H]	[I]	[J]	[K]	[L]	[M]	[N]	**[O]**	[P]	[Q]	[R]	[S]	[T]
10	[A]	[B]	[C]	[D]	**[E]**	[F]	[G]	[H]	[I]	[J]	[K]	[L]	[M]	[N]	[O]	[P]	[Q]	[R]	[S]	[T]
11	[A]	[B]	[C]	[D]	[E]	[F]	**[G]**	[H]	[I]	[J]	[K]	[L]	[M]	[N]	[O]	[P]	[Q]	[R]	[S]	[T]
12	[A]	**[B]**	[C]	[D]	[E]	[F]	[G]	[H]	[I]	[J]	[K]	[L]	[M]	[N]	[O]	[P]	[Q]	[R]	[S]	[T]
13	[A]	[B]	[C]	[D]	[E]	**[F]**	[G]	[H]	[I]	[J]	[K]	[L]	[M]	[N]	[O]	[P]	[Q]	[R]	[S]	[T]
14	[A]	[B]	[C]	[D]	[E]	[F]	[G]	**[H]**	[I]	[J]	[K]	[L]	[M]	[N]	[O]	[P]	[Q]	[R]	[S]	[T]
15	[A]	[B]	[C]	[D]	**[E]**	[F]	[G]	[H]	[I]	[J]	[K]	[L]	[M]	[N]	[O]	[P]	[Q]	[R]	[S]	[T]
16	[A]	[B]	[C]	[D]	[E]	[F]	**[G]**	[H]	[I]	[J]	[K]	[L]	[M]	[N]	[O]	[P]	[Q]	[R]	[S]	[T]
17	[A]	[B]	[C]	[D]	[E]	[F]	[G]	[H]	[I]	[J]	**[K]**	[L]	[M]	[N]	[O]	[P]	[Q]	[R]	[S]	[T]
18	[A]	**[B]**	[C]	[D]	[E]	[F]	[G]	[H]	[I]	[J]	[K]	[L]	[M]	[N]	[O]	[P]	[Q]	[R]	[S]	[T]
19	[A]	[B]	[C]	[D]	[E]	[F]	[G]	[H]	**[I]**	[J]	[K]	[L]	[M]	[N]	[O]	[P]	[Q]	[R]	[S]	[T]
20	[A]	[B]	[C]	[D]	**[E]**	[F]	[G]	[H]	[I]	[J]	[K]	[L]	[M]	[N]	[O]	[P]	[Q]	[R]	[S]	[T]

Standalone EMQ paper 2 (paper 2 type – Chapter 7)

1	[A]	[B]	[C]	[D]	[E]	**[F]**	[G]	[H]	[I]	[J]	[K]	[L]	[M]	[N]	[O]	[P]	[Q]	[R]	[S]	[T]
2	[A]	[B]	[C]	**[D]**	[E]	[F]	[G]	[H]	[I]	[J]	[K]	[L]	[M]	[N]	[O]	[P]	[Q]	[R]	[S]	[T]
3	**[A]**	[B]	[C]	[D]	[E]	[F]	[G]	[H]	[I]	[J]	[K]	[L]	[M]	[N]	[O]	[P]	[Q]	[R]	[S]	[T]
4	**[A]**	[B]	[C]	[D]	[E]	[F]	[G]	[H]	[I]	[J]	[K]	[L]	[M]	[N]	[O]	[P]	[Q]	[R]	[S]	[T]
5	[A]	[B]	[C]	[D]	[E]	**[F]**	[G]	[H]	[I]	[J]	[K]	[L]	[M]	[N]	[O]	[P]	[Q]	[R]	[S]	[T]
6	[A]	[B]	[C]	[D]	[E]	**[F]**	[G]	[H]	[I]	[J]	[K]	[L]	[M]	[N]	[O]	[P]	[Q]	[R]	[S]	[T]
7	**[A]**	[B]	[C]	[D]	[E]	[F]	[G]	[H]	[I]	[J]	[K]	[L]	[M]	[N]	[O]	[P]	[Q]	[R]	[S]	[T]
8	[A]	[B]	**[C]**	[D]	[E]	[F]	[G]	[H]	[I]	[J]	[K]	[L]	[M]	[N]	[O]	[P]	[Q]	[R]	[S]	[T]
9	[A]	[B]	[C]	[D]	**[E]**	[F]	[G]	[H]	[I]	[J]	[K]	[L]	[M]	[N]	[O]	[P]	[Q]	[R]	[S]	[T]
10	[A]	[B]	[C]	[D]	[E]	[F]	[G]	[H]	[I]	[J]	[K]	**[L]**	[M]	[N]	[O]	[P]	[Q]	[R]	[S]	[T]
11	[A]	[B]	[C]	**[D]**	[E]	[F]	[G]	[H]	[I]	[J]	[K]	[L]	[M]	[N]	[O]	[P]	[Q]	[R]	[S]	[T]
12	[A]	[B]	**[C]**	[D]	[E]	[F]	[G]	[H]	[I]	[J]	[K]	[L]	[M]	[N]	[O]	[P]	[Q]	[R]	[S]	[T]
13	[A]	[B]	[C]	[D]	[E]	[F]	[G]	[H]	[I]	[J]	[K]	[L]	[M]	[N]	**[O]**	[P]	[Q]	[R]	[S]	[T]
14	[A]	[B]	[C]	[D]	[E]	[F]	[G]	[H]	[I]	[J]	[K]	[L]	[M]	**[N]**	[O]	[P]	[Q]	[R]	[S]	[T]
15	[A]	[B]	[C]	[D]	[E]	**[F]**	[G]	[H]	[I]	[J]	[K]	[L]	[M]	[N]	[O]	[P]	[Q]	[R]	[S]	[T]
16	[A]	[B]	[C]	[D]	[E]	[F]	[G]	**[H]**	[I]	[J]	[K]	[L]	[M]	[N]	[O]	[P]	[Q]	[R]	[S]	[T]
17	[A]	**[B]**	[C]	[D]	[E]	[F]	[G]	[H]	[I]	[J]	[K]	[L]	[M]	[N]	[O]	[P]	[Q]	[R]	[S]	[T]
18	[A]	[B]	[C]	**[D]**	[E]	[F]	[G]	[H]	[I]	[J]	[K]	[L]	[M]	[N]	[O]	[P]	[Q]	[R]	[S]	[T]
19	[A]	[B]	[C]	[D]	[E]	[F]	[G]	**[H]**	[I]	[J]	[K]	[L]	[M]	[N]	[O]	[P]	[Q]	[R]	[S]	[T]
20	**[A]**	[B]	[C]	[D]	[E]	[F]	[G]	[H]	[I]	[J]	[K]	[L]	[M]	[N]	[O]	[P]	[Q]	[R]	[S]	[T]

Standalone EMQ paper 3 (paper 1 type – Chapter 8)

1	[A]	[B]	[C]	[D]	[E]	[F]	[G]	**[H]**	[I]	[J]	[K]	[L]	[M]	[N]	[O]	[P]	[Q]	[R]	[S]	[T]
2	[A]	[B]	**[C]**	[D]	[E]	[F]	[G]	[H]	[I]	[J]	[K]	[L]	[M]	[N]	[O]	[P]	[Q]	[R]	[S]	[T]
3	[A]	[B]	**[C]**	[D]	[E]	[F]	[G]	[H]	[I]	[J]	[K]	[L]	[M]	[N]	[O]	[P]	[Q]	[R]	[S]	[T]
4	[A]	**[B]**	[C]	[D]	[E]	[F]	[G]	[H]	[I]	[J]	[K]	[L]	[M]	[N]	[O]	[P]	[Q]	[R]	[S]	[T]
5	[A]	**[B]**	[C]	[D]	[E]	[F]	[G]	[H]	[I]	[J]	[K]	[L]	[M]	[N]	[O]	[P]	[Q]	[R]	[S]	[T]
6	[A]	[B]	**[C]**	[D]	[E]	[F]	[G]	[H]	[I]	[J]	[K]	[L]	[M]	[N]	[O]	[P]	[Q]	[R]	[S]	[T]
7	[A]	[B]	[C]	[D]	[E]	[F]	[G]	[H]	**[I]**	[J]	[K]	[L]	[M]	[N]	[O]	[P]	[Q]	[R]	[S]	[T]
8	[A]	[B]	[C]	**[D]**	[E]	[F]	[G]	[H]	[I]	[J]	[K]	[L]	[M]	[N]	[O]	[P]	[Q]	[R]	[S]	[T]
9	[A]	[B]	[C]	[D]	[E]	[F]	[G]	[H]	**[I]**	[J]	[K]	[L]	[M]	[N]	[O]	[P]	[Q]	[R]	[S]	[T]
10	[A]	[B]	**[C]**	[D]	[E]	[F]	[G]	[H]	[I]	[J]	[K]	[L]	[M]	[N]	[O]	[P]	[Q]	[R]	[S]	[T]
11	[A]	[B]	[C]	[D]	[E]	[F]	[G]	[H]	[I]	[J]	[K]	[L]	[M]	**[N]**	[O]	[P]	[Q]	[R]	[S]	[T]
12	[A]	[B]	[C]	[D]	[E]	[F]	**[G]**	[H]	[I]	[J]	[K]	[L]	[M]	[N]	[O]	[P]	[Q]	[R]	[S]	[T]
13	[A]	[B]	[C]	[D]	[E]	[F]	[G]	[H]	[I]	[J]	[K]	[L]	[M]	[N]	[O]	[P]	**[Q]**	[R]	[S]	[T]
14	[A]	[B]	[C]	[D]	**[E]**	[F]	[G]	[H]	[I]	[J]	[K]	[L]	[M]	[N]	[O]	[P]	[Q]	[R]	[S]	[T]
15	[A]	[B]	[C]	[D]	[E]	[F]	[G]	[H]	[I]	[J]	[K]	[L]	[M]	**[N]**	[O]	[P]	[Q]	[R]	[S]	[T]
16	[A]	[B]	[C]	[D]	[E]	[F]	[G]	[H]	[I]	**[J]**	[K]	[L]	[M]	[N]	[O]	[P]	[Q]	[R]	[S]	[T]
17	[A]	[B]	**[C]**	[D]	[E]	[F]	[G]	[H]	[I]	[J]	[K]	[L]	[M]	[N]	[O]	[P]	[Q]	[R]	[S]	[T]
18	[A]	[B]	[C]	[D]	[E]	[F]	**[G]**	[H]	[I]	[J]	[K]	[L]	[M]	[N]	[O]	[P]	[Q]	[R]	[S]	[T]
19	[A]	**[B]**	[C]	[D]	[E]	[F]	[G]	[H]	[I]	[J]	[K]	[L]	[M]	[N]	[O]	[P]	[Q]	[R]	[S]	[T]
20	[A]	[B]	[C]	[D]	[E]	[F]	**[G]**	[H]	[I]	[J]	[K]	[L]	[M]	[N]	[O]	[P]	[Q]	[R]	[S]	[T]

Standalone EMQ paper 4 (paper 2 type – Chapter 9)

1 [A] [B] [C] [D] **[E]** [F] [G] [H] [I] [J] [K] [L] [M] [N] [O] [P] [Q] [R] [S] [T]

2 **[A]** [B] [C] [D] [E] [F] [G] [H] [I] [J] [K] [L] [M] [N] [O] [P] [Q] [R] [S] [T]

3 [A] [B] [C] [D] **[E]** [F] [G] [H] [I] [J] [K] [L] [M] [N] [O] [P] [Q] [R] [S] [T]

4 [A] [B] [C] **[D]** [E] [F] [G] [H] [I] [J] [K] [L] [M] [N] [O] [P] [Q] [R] [S] [T]

5 [A] **[B]** [C] [D] [E] [F] [G] [H] [I] [J] [K] [L] [M] [N] [O] [P] [Q] [R] [S] [T]

6 [A] [B] [C] [D] [E] [F] [G] [H] [I] **[J]** [K] [L] [M] [N] [O] [P] [Q] [R] [S] [T]

7 [A] [B] [C] [D] [E] [F] [G] [H] [I] [J] [K] **[L]** [M] [N] [O] [P] [Q] [R] [S] [T]

8 [A] [B] [C] [D] **[E]** [F] [G] [H] [I] [J] [K] [L] [M] [N] [O] [P] [Q] [R] [S] [T]

9 [A] [B] [C] [D] [E] [F] [G] [H] [I] [J] [K] [L] [M] **[N]** [O] [P] [Q] [R] [S] [T]

10 [A] [B] [C] [D] [E] **[F]** [G] [H] [I] [J] [K] [L] [M] [N] [O] [P] [Q] [R] [S] [T]

11 **[A]** [B] [C] [D] [E] [F] [G] [H] [I] [J] [K] [L] [M] [N] [O] [P] [Q] [R] [S] [T]

12 **[A]** [B] [C] [D] [E] [F] [G] [H] [I] [J] [K] [L] [M] [N] [O] [P] [Q] [R] [S] [T]

13 [A] [B] [C] [D] [E] [F] [G] **[H]** [I] [J] [K] [L] [M] [N] [O] [P] [Q] [R] [S] [T]

14 [A] [B] [C] [D] [E] [F] [G] [H] [I] **[J]** [K] [L] [M] [N] [O] [P] [Q] [R] [S] [T]

15 [A] [B] [C] [D] [E] [F] [G] [H] [I] [J] [K] [L] [M] [N] [O] **[P]** [Q] [R] [S] [T]

16 [A] [B] **[C]** [D] [E] [F] [G] [H] [I] [J] [K] [L] [M] [N] [O] [P] [Q] [R] [S] [T]

17 [A] **[B]** [C] [D] [E] [F] [G] [H] [I] [J] [K] [L] [M] [N] [O] [P] [Q] [R] [S] [T]

18 **[A]** [B] [C] [D] [E] [F] [G] [H] [I] [J] [K] [L] [M] [N] [O] [P] [Q] [R] [S] [T]

19 [A] [B] [C] [D] [E] [F] [G] [H] **[I]** [J] [K] [L] [M] [N] [O] [P] [Q] [R] [S] [T]

20 [A] **[B]** [C] [D] [E] [F] [G] [H] [I] [J] [K] [L] [M] [N] [O] [P] [Q] [R] [S] [T]

1	[A]	[B]	[C]	[D]	[E]	[F]	[G]	[H]	[I]	[J]	[K]	[L]	[M]	[N]	[O]	[P]	[Q]	[R]	[S]	[T]
2	[A]	[B]	[C]	[D]	[E]	[F]	[G]	[H]	[I]	[J]	[K]	[L]	[M]	[N]	[O]	[P]	[Q]	[R]	[S]	[T]
3	[A]	[B]	[C]	[D]	[E]	[F]	[G]	[H]	[I]	[J]	[K]	[L]	[M]	[N]	[O]	[P]	[Q]	[R]	[S]	[T]
4	[A]	[B]	[C]	[D]	[E]	[F]	[G]	[H]	[I]	[J]	[K]	[L]	[M]	[N]	[O]	[P]	[Q]	[R]	[S]	[T]
5	[A]	[B]	[C]	[D]	[E]	[F]	[G]	[H]	[I]	[J]	[K]	[L]	[M]	[N]	[O]	[P]	[Q]	[R]	[S]	[T]
6	[A]	[B]	[C]	[D]	[E]	[F]	[G]	[H]	[I]	[J]	[K]	[L]	[M]	[N]	[O]	[P]	[Q]	[R]	[S]	[T]
7	[A]	[B]	[C]	[D]	[E]	[F]	[G]	[H]	[I]	[J]	[K]	[L]	[M]	[N]	[O]	[P]	[Q]	[R]	[S]	[T]
8	[A]	[B]	[C]	[D]	[E]	[F]	[G]	[H]	[I]	[J]	[K]	[L]	[M]	[N]	[O]	[P]	[Q]	[R]	[S]	[T]
9	[A]	[B]	[C]	[D]	[E]	[F]	[G]	[H]	[I]	[J]	[K]	[L]	[M]	[N]	[O]	[P]	[Q]	[R]	[S]	[T]
10	[A]	[B]	[C]	[D]	[E]	[F]	[G]	[H]	[I]	[J]	[K]	[L]	[M]	[N]	[O]	[P]	[Q]	[R]	[S]	[T]

11	[A]	[B]	[C]	[D]	[E]	[F]	[G]	[H]	[I]	[J]	[K]	[L]	[M]	[N]	[O]	[P]	[Q]	[R]	[S]	[T]
12	[A]	[B]	[C]	[D]	[E]	[F]	[G]	[H]	[I]	[J]	[K]	[L]	[M]	[N]	[O]	[P]	[Q]	[R]	[S]	[T]
13	[A]	[B]	[C]	[D]	[E]	[F]	[G]	[H]	[I]	[J]	[K]	[L]	[M]	[N]	[O]	[P]	[Q]	[R]	[S]	[T]
14	[A]	[B]	[C]	[D]	[E]	[F]	[G]	[H]	[I]	[J]	[K]	[L]	[M]	[N]	[O]	[P]	[Q]	[R]	[S]	[T]
15	[A]	[B]	[C]	[D]	[E]	[F]	[G]	[H]	[I]	[J]	[K]	[L]	[M]	[N]	[O]	[P]	[Q]	[R]	[S]	[T]
16	[A]	[B]	[C]	[D]	[E]	[F]	[G]	[H]	[I]	[J]	[K]	[L]	[M]	[N]	[O]	[P]	[Q]	[R]	[S]	[T]
17	[A]	[B]	[C]	[D]	[E]	[F]	[G]	[H]	[I]	[J]	[K]	[L]	[M]	[N]	[O]	[P]	[Q]	[R]	[S]	[T]
18	[A]	[B]	[C]	[D]	[E]	[F]	[G]	[H]	[I]	[J]	[K]	[L]	[M]	[N]	[O]	[P]	[Q]	[R]	[S]	[T]
19	[A]	[B]	[C]	[D]	[E]	[F]	[G]	[H]	[I]	[J]	[K]	[L]	[M]	[N]	[O]	[P]	[Q]	[R]	[S]	[T]
20	[A]	[B]	[C]	[D]	[E]	[F]	[G]	[H]	[I]	[J]	[K]	[L]	[M]	[N]	[O]	[P]	[Q]	[R]	[S]	[T]

Appendix 2
Blank answer sheets for the mock examinations

Please feel free to photocopy these so that you can easily use and reuse them.

Appendix 2
EMQ section of full papers and for EMQ standalone papers

Complete by fully filling in with pencil the lozenge corresponding to the **single** correct answer.

	A	B	C	D	E
21	[T]	[T]	[T]	[T]	[T]
	[F]	[F]	[F]	[F]	[F]
22	[T]	[T]	[T]	[T]	[T]
	[F]	[F]	[F]	[F]	[F]
23	[T]	[T]	[T]	[T]	[T]
	[F]	[F]	[F]	[F]	[F]
24	[T]	[T]	[T]	[T]	[T]
	[F]	[F]	[F]	[F]	[F]
25	[T]	[T]	[T]	[T]	[T]
	[F]	[F]	[F]	[F]	[F]
26	[T]	[T]	[T]	[T]	[T]
	[F]	[F]	[F]	[F]	[F]
27	[T]	[T]	[T]	[T]	[T]
	[F]	[F]	[F]	[F]	[F]
28	[T]	[T]	[T]	[T]	[T]
	[F]	[F]	[F]	[F]	[F]
29	[T]	[T]	[T]	[T]	[T]
	[F]	[F]	[F]	[F]	[F]
30	[T]	[T]	[T]	[T]	[T]
	[F]	[F]	[F]	[F]	[F]
31	[T]	[T]	[T]	[T]	[T]
	[F]	[F]	[F]	[F]	[F]
32	[T]	[T]	[T]	[T]	[T]
	[F]	[F]	[F]	[F]	[F]

	A	B	C	D	E
33	[T]	[T]	[T]	[T]	[T]
	[F]	[F]	[F]	[F]	[F]
34	[T]	[T]	[T]	[T]	[T]
	[F]	[F]	[F]	[F]	[F]
35	[T]	[T]	[T]	[T]	[T]
	[F]	[F]	[F]	[F]	[F]
36	[T]	[T]	[T]	[T]	[T]
	[F]	[F]	[F]	[F]	[F]
37	[T]	[T]	[T]	[T]	[T]
	[F]	[F]	[F]	[F]	[F]
38	[T]	[T]	[T]	[T]	[T]
	[F]	[F]	[F]	[F]	[F]
39	[T]	[T]	[T]	[T]	[T]
	[F]	[F]	[F]	[F]	[F]
40	[T]	[T]	[T]	[T]	[T]
	[F]	[F]	[F]	[F]	[F]
41	[T]	[T]	[T]	[T]	[T]
	[F]	[F]	[F]	[F]	[F]
42	[T]	[T]	[T]	[T]	[T]
	[F]	[F]	[F]	[F]	[F]
43	[T]	[T]	[T]	[T]	[T]
	[F]	[F]	[F]	[F]	[F]
44	[T]	[T]	[T]	[T]	[T]
	[F]	[F]	[F]	[F]	[F]

	A	B	C	D	E
45	[T]	[T]	[T]	[T]	[T]
	[F]	[F]	[F]	[F]	[F]
46	[T]	[T]	[T]	[T]	[T]
	[F]	[F]	[F]	[F]	[F]
47	[T]	[T]	[T]	[T]	[T]
	[F]	[F]	[F]	[F]	[F]
48	[T]	[T]	[T]	[T]	[T]
	[F]	[F]	[F]	[F]	[F]
49	[T]	[T]	[T]	[T]	[T]
	[F]	[F]	[F]	[F]	[F]
50	[T]	[T]	[T]	[T]	[T]
	[F]	[F]	[F]	[F]	[F]
51	[T]	[T]	[T]	[T]	[T]
	[F]	[F]	[F]	[F]	[F]
52	[T]	[T]	[T]	[T]	[T]
	[F]	[F]	[F]	[F]	[F]
53	[T]	[T]	[T]	[T]	[T]
	[F]	[F]	[F]	[F]	[F]
54	[T]	[T]	[T]	[T]	[T]
	[F]	[F]	[F]	[F]	[F]
55	[T]	[T]	[T]	[T]	[T]
	[F]	[F]	[F]	[F]	[F]
56	[T]	[T]	[T]	[T]	[T]
	[F]	[F]	[F]	[F]	[F]

	A	B	C	D	E
57	[T]	[T]	[T]	[T]	[T]
	[F]	[F]	[F]	[F]	[F]
58	[T]	[T]	[T]	[T]	[T]
	[F]	[F]	[F]	[F]	[F]
59	[T]	[T]	[T]	[T]	[T]
	[F]	[F]	[F]	[F]	[F]
60	[T]	[T]	[T]	[T]	[T]
	[F]	[F]	[F]	[F]	[F]
61	[T]	[T]	[T]	[T]	[T]
	[F]	[F]	[F]	[F]	[F]
62	[T]	[T]	[T]	[T]	[T]
	[F]	[F]	[F]	[F]	[F]
63	[T]	[T]	[T]	[T]	[T]
	[F]	[F]	[F]	[F]	[F]
64	[T]	[T]	[T]	[T]	[T]
	[F]	[F]	[F]	[F]	[F]
65	[T]	[T]	[T]	[T]	[T]
	[F]	[F]	[F]	[F]	[F]
66	[T]	[T]	[T]	[T]	[T]
	[F]	[F]	[F]	[F]	[F]
67	[T]	[T]	[T]	[T]	[T]
	[F]	[F]	[F]	[F]	[F]
68	[T]	[T]	[T]	[T]	[T]
	[F]	[F]	[F]	[F]	[F]

Index